How to Give Cheerfully without Tithing

T.S. Cairns

Published by

GOOD NEWS FELLOWSHIP MINISTRIES

220 Sleepy Creek Rd.

Macon, GA 31210

Phone: (478) 757-8071

Table of Contents

Special Thanks

There are many people who have helped in the development of this book. I would like to thank these people especially for their help:

My beautiful wife Tania who checked my work, gave many wonderful suggestions and put up with my long periods of absence.

My champion son Caleb who also had to put up with not having as much time with me as he would like.

My brother Phil who gave up his time to edit and make excellent suggestions for the book.

My brother to another mother, Gavin Tooley who also gave up his time to edit and make great suggestions.

Kathie Walters who gave me some stories and lovingly kicked me into action to get the book written.

I'd also like to thank Jesus because He did it all.

Introduction

I love giving. I get nearly as excited when I give in church as when I'm buying presents for my family. I get to see the expression on my family's face when I give to them and I love that. I don't always get to see it when I give in church.

I haven't always been this way though.

Let me make it clear that I'm not a 'Gifts' person. I know people who go into raptures when their cat brings them a dead mouse. It was a gift; the cat must love them! This isn't me. I forgot my *own* birthday one year. Gift giving and receiving isn't really my 'thing.' If my cat could tell me how awesome I was, that would be a different story.

My wife loves giving too. But she's not a 'Gifts' person. I mean, she likes gifts, but she doesn't '*like*' gifts. One Christmas, my son bought Tania a kettle. It was the most expensive kettle on the shelves. *I* didn't think the kettle was a good idea but my son was a determined thirteen year old.

I made a rule never to give my wife any kitchen related objects as presents after I saw what happened when my father bought my mother a frying pan with a brush and dust pan wrapped up in it. The dent in the pan was never repaired but at least they stayed married.

When Tania opened the present and saw the kettle I could tell she wasn't that impressed. Before she could say anything, I started explaining how hard Caleb had looked for just the right present.

I told her how much he thought about what she liked. I also told her how hard he looked to find something attractive and useful. Caleb knew his mum liked tea and coffee (especially when I make it for her). Tania's eyes softened. It wasn't the gift itself she liked, it was the time and effort that went into finding the gift that was important.

The reason I'm saying this is because you don't have to be a certain 'Type' of person to love giving. Becoming a cheerful giver instead of a tither does not require a change in your personality. It's not something you have to force yourself to become or follow certain rules to achieve. In fact, it's quite the opposite.

I grew up in a church that believed in tithing. My parents tithed and they taught me to tithe. I put aside ten percent of any pocket money I was given or any money I earned. It was a practice I continued well into adulthood.

As a child I didn't understand what I was doing, only that tithing was what all people who loved God did. I was told that giving ten percent to God was good and not giving it was bad. I didn't know why God needed my twenty cents more than I needed a mixed bag of lollies, but I put that money in the plate each week anyway.

As I got older I discovered that giving in church was far more complex than what I originally thought. Most 'New Christian' courses I did had an entire chapter on tithes and offerings. And I had to do the 'New Christians' course in every new church I went to. Almost every course said that if I gave my tithes and offerings I would be blessed and if I didn't, I would be cursed.

I wrestled with the issue of tithing on the net or gross. I was taught that if I tithed and didn't get money back I must have been tithing with the wrong attitude. I changed my attitude. I was told that if I wasn't being blessed and I was tithing I mustn't be giving enough, so I gave more.

I was told that it was a lack of faith that hindered the blessing of God, so I prayed for more faith and stepped boldly out giving more than I was able, believing for a hundred fold increase. I never received it.

I learned that simply giving the ten percent was not enough. I had to give an offering. This was because the tithe opened up the windows of heaven and offerings cause the blessing to pour out.

I tithed and gave and still things broke down. I gave even when there were bills to pay and no money came back to meet the mounting bills. I was told to keep tithing because this is what would cause God to bless me and I just had to have faith.

I was told that it was important to keep money coming into the 'House of God.' If I gave faithfully, looking after God's House, He would look after mine. None of what I learnt seemed to work.

A number of years ago, God took me on a journey of discovering Grace. He challenged my belief in tithing and I researched the Bible, other books and the internet to find out what it said about giving, tithing and offerings.

For a while, I wavered between tithing and not tithing. When I didn't tithe I lived in fear of God's curse. When I did tithe, I stressed over finances and lived miserably.

I finally concluded that giving was not about putting the mandatory ten percent of any money I received into a bag or plate. It was about being free and generous with the finances God had entrusted me with. I became a giver instead of a tither.

This belief was particularly scary for me, because soon after this discovery, I began to run a church. If I couldn't tithe, then I couldn't ask my congregation to. I had to wonder where my income would come from.

I faced opposition to my belief. I was told my theology was wrong and that I should go back and research again. I had other people who were scared on my behalf. They didn't want me to set a standard and then have to go back on it, destroying the congregation's faith in my ability to lead.

I was swayed back and forth, questioning *my* right to question a practice that was held by so many esteemed scholars and ministers of the gospel. Who was I to disagree with such a well-established tradition?

I finally resolved to give under Grace, and encourage the church I led to do the same. So I gave, as directed by the Holy Spirit, generously, extravagantly and freely. I didn't limit myself to a percentage.

I began to give based on faith in God's ability to provide, His willingness to give and His unconditional love for me. I began to give under Grace instead of Law and in this place I gave cheerfully with miracle provision.

This book outlines the results of my research on this subject carried out over seven years. I know that as you read it, you will also discover the way to give in freedom, with joy and with blessing. Enjoy the journey.

Chapter 1: How I Gave

God Is A Giver But The Devil Doesn't Want You To Know

At the outset, I'd like to reinforce that I believe in giving and I love giving. I also believe in financially supporting the local body of believers we belong to. I believe that most pastors who teach tithing do so with the best of intentions for their congregations.

I believe that the more we take on the character of Christ, the more abundantly generous we will become.

God the Father is a giver. He holds nothing back from us. He didn't even spare His own Son. He is a good provider. The enemy wants you to believe that God is holding back, and this was the lie he told Adam and Eve in the Garden of Eden. Grab the fruit and you will become like gods.

They were already made in the image of God.

The enemy sowed doubt into the minds of Adam and Eve about the Father's willingness to provide. This is the same doubt that afflicts us today. If I give everything that God is asking me to, will He provide for me, will He hold back?

That doubt will cause *us* to hold back. Fear will stop us from being as free as we are meant to be. Reliance on material possessions will stop us from abandoning ourselves to God.

Reliance on the Holy Spirit allows us to be free in our giving.

> *"... where the Spirit of the Lord is, there is liberty." 2 Corinthians 3:17*

If we're not free, we can't give with real cheerfulness.

The challenge of the New Testament is that we move from ritualistic behaviours that satisfy the demands of the law, to heart attitudes that exemplify the character of the Father. It is made very clear to us that righteousness comes from faith not ritual behaviours (works).

I'd like you to try something. Try not tithing or giving for a period of time. Ask yourself how you feel about it. What thoughts does not tithing set up in your mind?

Do you feel fear? Do you feel that God will be angry with you? Do you think the blessing will stop?

The answers to those questions can tell you whether or not you're giving from faith. The way you react to not tithing can let you know whether you are giving from a place of intimacy with the Father or out of religious duty. Try it and see how you respond.

God loves you because of who He is, not because of what you do. Your giving is not going to cause God to be more willing to do good things for you. Your works, including giving, will not make you righteous. Only Jesus can do that. God will not love you less if you don't tithe. Can you agree with that?

Our giving must come from faith as well as attitudes that exemplify the heart of the Father.

> *"Every good gift and every perfect gift is from above, and comes down from the Father of lights, with whom there is no variation or shadow of turning." James 1:17*

> *"If you then, being evil, know how to give good gifts to your children, how much more will your Father who is in Heaven give good things to those who ask Him." Matthew 7:11*

Every father I've met lights up when they talk about the good things they've given to their children. The reason for this is because giving to our children is an area where we are like God. God loves giving His children good things and because we are like Him, made in His image, we love giving our children good things.

God loves giving so we love giving. God doesn't hold back so we don't hold back. To not love giving means that something, somewhere, is out of alignment with the Spirit of God.

"The tithe is Mine," saith the Lord

When I first embarked on this journey I had a chat with a friend. I wasn't sure where he stood on giving but I trusted his Biblical understanding. He told me he didn't tithe any more. I took an involuntary step away from him expecting some sudden evil to befall him.

He shared this experience that started him on the same journey as me.

He went to an ATM before church to get the tithe out. He felt God say to him to keep it. He immediately assumed it was the devil, because God wouldn't say such heretical things.

God told him again, 'Keep the tithe.'

"But God," he said. "I can't keep the tithe."

God asked him "Why not?"

"Well," my friend sputtered. "Because it's yours. I can't keep what belongs to you."

"So the tithe is mine then?" Asked God.

"Absolutely," said my friend.

"If the tithe is mine," asked God. "Can't I do what I want with it?"

"Yes," replied my friend. "You're God. You can do what You want with anything."

"Good," said God. "What I want to do with the tithe is for you to keep it."

God won that discussion and later that week, my friend had something go wrong with his car. He just happened to have enough to pay for it because he kept the tithe. After using the tithe to pay for the car repairs, my friend spent the next week waiting for the lightening bolt to strike him down. It never came.

That story was true. Something else that was true, but wasn't funny was the fact that my friend felt he couldn't talk to anyone about what he believed. He felt that no-one would understand what he meant when he said he didn't tithe.

He was very generous. I knew he gave a lot to our church, to other charitable organisations and to people he saw in need, but he didn't tithe.

It seemed to him that tithing was seen as a sign of a person's commitment to the church. He felt that others thought not tithing meant he wasn't committed to the church, the vision or the leadership. He felt he wouldn't be trusted as much as those who did tithe.

Is tithing really Biblical?

So what is "Tithing?" If you have been around most mainstream denominational churches for any length of time the word will have come up.

Tithing, as most people understand it, is **the regular giving of ten percent of a person's income**, however obtained, (weekly, fortnightly or monthly) into the church they attend. The income could result from the sale of a house or car, a business venture, wages, salary or pension, an insurance payout or inheritance, a tax return or any other way money has come into your hands.

Some say it is obligatory, some say it is not and others say it is the minimum requirement in order to have the blessings of God. Lately, instead of using the word tithing, the word 'Firstfruits' has been substituted. 'Firstfruits' in the Old Testament always referred to what was used for various offerings. In the New Testament, 'Firstfruits' refers primarily to people and never money. I haven't found a connection between tithing and 'Firstfruits.'

I grew up tithing and I believed it was obligatory. I would tithe on any source of finances that came into my possession, including financial gifts. I believed that tithing would open the door for God's blessing over my life and that not tithing would open the door for the devil to wreak havoc in my life. I believed that ten percent of whatever money came into my possession was God's and that the ninety percent left was mine to do what I needed to with it.

But is tithing, as it is presented today, Biblical? Is a lack of financial blessing around our lives really the result of coming under the curse of Malachi chapter 3? What is the Biblical standard of giving? Is there a minimum requirement? Is tithing an undisputed principle that has passed from the Old Testament into the New Testament?

Chapter 2: How They Gave Before The Law

Tithes, Offerings, And Circumcision

One of the most commonly cited reasons why people believe tithing is for today, is because Abram (Abraham) tithed before the Law. This is found in Genesis 14 and is one of two times that tithing is mentioned before the Law was instituted for Israel.

The date when The Law was introduced has been estimated as being between 1500 and 1200 BCE (Before Common Era). Young Earth creationists would say there is a time period of between 2,500 and nearly 3,000 years of history between creation and the giving of The Law. In all that time, tithing is mentioned twice in the Bible.

The theory says that because Abram paid a tithe to Melchizedek before the Law was instituted then we should continue paying tithes. If he tithed before the Law, then tithing is not really under the Law and so we should tithe as well.

Well, tithes *were* paid before the Law, so should we continue to pay tithes because they were not under Law when the practice was first demonstrated? Are two mentions of an occurrence over a period of 3,000 years enough to say a principle was established? Is there evidence that tithing was passed on from father to son over many generations?

In truth, offerings and circumcision are mentioned more often than tithing. Circumcision is a practise that is shown to have been passed on from father to son (Genesis 34). If tithing can be preached on as a practice that was firmly established before the Law because of two mentions, why is it spoken of more often than offerings? And why is circumcision not mentioned at all, except in the occasional reference to the spiritual condition of the heart?

Both of these practices are mentioned more often than tithing and are shown to be practices passed on to the next generation, while tithing is not. Giving before the law far more commonly took the form of free will offerings. Even then, as the incident with Cain and

Abel shows us, God is more interested in the attitude of the heart than He is in the actual offering itself.

Abram and Melchizedek

So let's look at the exchange between Abram and Melchizedek. This event is also discussed by the author of Hebrews in Hebrews 7. We need to examine the circumstances, or the context of this tithe.

We read in Genesis 14 that Abram gave a tithe (or a tenth) of all he had. Hebrews 7 expands on that to say that he gave a tenth of the spoils.

The story says that four kings got together to ravage the surrounding lands. A group of five kings joined together to try to stop them. They failed. In the process, the first group of kings took people and goods to divide among themselves.

Unfortunately, Lot, the nephew of Abram, was in the group of people who were taken captive. When Abram heard about it, he gathered his three hundred and eighteen trained servants together, a few of his allies and went out to defeat the four kings. This he did with outstanding success. They rescued Lot, his family and all of Lot's goods as well as all that the four kings had taken.

On the way back from the battle, Abram passed through Salem (Jerusalem) and was met by Melchizedek, King of Salem and priest of God Most High. Melchizedek brought out bread and wine and blessed Abram. After the blessing, Abram gave Melchizedek a tenth (tithe) of all he had.

Again, the author of Hebrews clarifies this and explains that it was a tenth or tithe of the spoils. It is possible that, as a tithe was often used as a measure in taxation systems or levies at the time, the tenth was given to the King of Salem as a levy or a sign of good intentions while passing through the area.

But the story does not end there, and it is important to look at the story in its whole context.

When Abram returns to the five kings, the king of Sodom addresses him. He tells Abram that he can keep all the goods (the spoils of war) that had originally belonged to the five kings, however, the kings wanted their people back.

Abram responds by saying that he wouldn't take any of the goods either, as he didn't want people saying that the kings had made him rich. He wanted people to know that it was the Lord, God most High who had made him rich.

But the story still does not stop there. Abram goes on to say that what he would keep were the supplies his men had eaten. This of course makes sense, but note he didn't offer to pay for the supplies that were used. He also said that his allies who went with him could keep their portion if they wanted. That was up to them. *That* is the end of the story.

Abram's tithe wasn't from his money

Now let's just think of goods as money for a moment. Just pretend you were robbed. The thieves stole $1,000 off you. Who does that $1,000 belong to? You or the thieves? They may think it's theirs, but you know it's yours.

Just pretend for a moment that a friend of yours meets you and says that he will get your money back. Your friend grabs a couple of his friends and goes after the thieves to get your money. Who does your friend think the $1,000 belongs to? You, the thieves or him and his friends? You would hope he knows it's yours.

Your friend is successful and retrieves the money. On the way home he stops and buys $50 worth of take-away food for his friends and himself. He notices a church across the road and goes to confess his violence. The priest blesses him and then your friend gives the priest $100 (a tenth or tithe of the $1000). Your friend gets back and gives your $850 to you.

You offer to pay him for his services but he refuses. He says for you to ask his friends if they want any money. Whatever arrangement you make with them is between you and them.

The question then is, whose money did your friend give a tithe of? Was it your friend's money, the thieves' money or was it yours? Whose goods did Abram give a tithe of? Were the goods his, the four kings or the five kings? The important question is, who did Abram believe they belonged to? The answer to that is found in Genesis 14:23:

> *"... I will not take anything that is **yours**..."*
> *(emphasis is mine)*

Abram saw that the goods belonged to the King of Sodom and the other four kings who had banded together. So he paid a tithe on someone else's goods. We never read in the Bible about Abram (Abraham) giving a tithe on his own increase.

We see him giving many offerings, including preparing to offer his own son. Isaac was not a tithe. Isaac was an offering of 100%. It was an offering of Abraham's future. There was no 10% with that sacrifice.

It was at the place of Abraham giving 100% that God was revealed as 'The Lord Will Provide.' It's at the place where we think we will lose it all (when following God's direction) that we find God to be the One who gives it all.

When Tania and I moved to the town we now live, to be pastors, we gave up our home. It was the second time we'd sold the house we owned to follow God's call. This house was an answer to prayer. It was a miracle house. It had everything we wanted and we were happy there. We believed the house was an investment for the future.

God called us away and we had to sell the house because we were unable to maintain the payments. At the time of writing this book we are renting a house to live in. But God is 'The Lord Will Provide.' We have an absolute assurance that God has a house for us and He will provide it.

The first time we sold our house to follow God's call, I didn't have that assurance. In fact I was pretty annoyed that God didn't do what I believed He should have done. I was trying to tithe but not doing it well. I was stressed, angry and very unpleasant to be around. I resented giving the tithe and coming home to see the amount of bills to be paid.

I had no freedom in giving and no joy. Now I give freely, joyously and I give more than I did before. I get to enjoy being a blessing to others without fear of lack for myself. I know that God is 'The Lord Will Provide.'

When we look at Abraham's life, we see that he consistently practiced offerings. The only time we read about him giving a tithe in his one hundred and seventy five years of life, he used someone else's goods to do it.

I think there would be much more joy in giving if tithing looked more like Abram's tithe. You only do it once in your life and when you do, you dip into someone else's purse or wallet for the money. Of course the joy might stop when you look in your own wallet after someone else has done the same thing. It depends on the revelation you have of God as 'The Lord Will Provide.'

Abram's tithe may have been under law

As was mentioned earlier, the Bible only mentions tithing twice before it is introduced in the Law as part of the Israelite tax system. Outside of the Bible, it was apparently fairly common.

"The widespread practice in the ancient world of tithing by giving a portion of one's profit or spoils of war extended from Greece to China. Donation of a tenth portion was common apparently because most people 'counted in tens, based on ten fingers."
(Elwell, 1996)

Abram came from Chaldea, part of Mesopotamia. Mesopotamia had a tithe system, which was basically a ten per cent tax system. The tithe was also demanded by the gods of Mesopotamia, including Chaldea, Assyria and Babylon. (Oppenheim et al. 1958, 368 -370)

What this means is that when Abram gave the tenth to Melchizedek, he *may* have done so in accordance with the law he had known under the Mesopotamian (Babylonian) monetary system.

So tithing, before the Levitical Law, was associated primarily with taxes, rather than giving to God. To be honest, I'm yet to find cheerfulness when working out my taxes. I'm sure that will change though.

Paul tells us to:

> *"Rejoice always, pray without ceasing, in everything give thanks; for this is the will of God in Christ Jesus for you." 1 Thessalonians 5: 16-18*

If it's God's will for me, then He will enable me to do it.

Abram was blessed before he tithed

There is another point to note when comparing Abram's tithe with the modern day version of the tithe. There are some people who say that if we give our tithe (and offering), it opens the door to blessing. Give first and then be blessed. Sow and then reap.

The problem here is that Abram was already blessed before he gave the tithe. We read in Genesis 13 that Abram was very rich in livestock, in silver and in gold.

Abram was so rich that when he came to the land of Canaan with Lot, there was not enough room for them to camp together. God had blessed Abram all along the journey from Chaldea, Egypt and into Canaan and that blessing was not dependent on him tithing. God promised Abram he would be blessed and God was faithful to fulfil His promise.

Should we really hold Abraham up as the example to follow in tithing outside of the Law? Perhaps not, since the one-off example he set was in fact completely different to the concept we have of tithing in modern society. If he did tithe before that, it would have been a tax and gone to a government, not a church.

The circumstances of Abraham's tithe also, in no way place any obligation on us to tithe.

If we were to look to Abraham for an example of giving then we would be better to take note of the free will offerings he made constantly to God. We should take note of the fact that Abraham was blessed before he gave a tithe. Abraham's blessing was not dependant on his actions but instead on the faithfulness, goodness and grace of God.

That in itself is a reason to have a little joy in giving. You will receive the promises and blessing of God, not because of what you do, but because of God's faithfulness to do what He said He would. It's not up to you. It's all Him.

Jacob's tithe

The other time tithing (giving a tenth) is mentioned before the introduction of the Levitical Law is in Genesis 28:

> *"Then Jacob made a vow, saying, 'If God will be with me, and keep me in this way that I am going, and give me bread to eat and clothing to put on, so that I come back to my father's house in peace, then the Lord shall be my God. And this stone which I have set as a pillar shall be God's house, and of all that You give me I will surely give a tenth to you.'" Genesis 28:20-22*

Here we see Jacob making a promise. We don't ever read if Jacob meets his end of the vow to give a tenth to God, but even if he did, the whole context of the vow is the opposite to the modern concept of tithing.

Some people are told to give the tithe, regardless of their circumstances. They are told to tithe before paying the bills and trust God to supply their needs. They are told to step out in faith, and that faith will activate the financial miracle.

They are told that as they tithe they will be blessed, but the tithe has to come first. To do anything else is to demonstrate a lack of faith in God. They are told not to wait for the miracle, but to sow into it.

Jacob's promise of a tithe is conditional. Not only does he say he will only give a tithe after God has come through with His promise of blessing, but he says he will only make the Lord his God if God comes through for him.

In essence, Jacob says to God, 'I'm not going to serve You or give anything to You until You have proven yourself to me.' This is opposite to what we are told about tithing today. We are never taught (and rightly so) that we should put conditions on God.

I don't advise anyone to put conditions on serving God. I've tried putting conditions on God and manipulating Him. Let's just say that things didn't work out so well with that.

Jacob doesn't negotiate well with God

One other thing to consider is that God promises Jacob incredible blessings in verses 13 to 15 of Genesis 28. They are unconditional. Nothing required of Jacob in order to receive them. If we compare God's promise with Jacob's vow we see that Jacob has renegotiated a reduction in blessing.

Instead of receiving the kinds of blessing that only God could provide, Jacob asks for the kinds of things he can achieve by his own efforts. He then tries to sweeten the deal for God by promising something in return.

Jacob lost with the promise of a tithe. God's promise of blessing was bigger and better than Jacob's requests. It was unconditional. It was based on the fact that God fulfils His promises and always binds Himself to a covenant He has made.

By faith, we are sons of Abraham and inheritors of the blessing.

> *"Therefore know that only those who are of the faith are sons of Abraham. So then those who are of faith are blessed with believing Abraham." Galatians 3:7, 9*

Why would we give away the greater, unconditional blessing for the lesser blessing dependent on the tithe?

Instead of living in the realm of faith that opens doors to receive provision from the eternal kingdom of God, Jacob chose to trust his own ability to provide for himself, and give something to God that came from a work of the flesh.

Unfortunately we often do a similar thing. We make money through the sweat of our brow (or the whirring of our grey matter) and give God a portion of what we have achieved in our flesh. I believe what God really wants is for us to place our trust in Him and give out of the abundance He provides for us from the resources of Heaven.

Our giving is meant to come through faith. When we have an absolute assurance that God will provide we can give cheerfully and joyously because there is no fear of lack.

To sum up

Tithing did occur before the introduction of the Law. However, the most accepted and common form of giving to God by Abraham was offerings. Other tithing in various nations was in the form of a mandatory taxation system.

Abraham's recorded tithe was actually using someone else's money. It was also a once off event. This is different to today's tithe which is **the regular giving of ten percent of your income, however obtained.**

Abraham offered all and Jacob offered 10%. Abraham found God as 'The Lord Will Provide' and Jacob's tithe promise was associated with a reduction of blessing but harder work.

Chapter 3: How They Gave Under The Law

Who Had To Tithe?

So what does tithing under the Mosaic or Levitical Law look like? How was the tithe paid? What was done with the tithe? Who had to pay the tithe? Where did the tithe have to be paid? How often was the tithe paid? Was the tithe all there was to pay? Does the Levitical tithe look like the modern day tithe?

There is much discussion about the tithe of the Old Testament. There are some who claim there were three tithes, totalling around 23 and 1/3% of the produce. There are others claiming that it is only 10% and others say it was 20%.

"And all the tithe of the land, whether of the seed of the land or of the fruit of the tree, is the Lord's. It is holy to the Lord." Leviticus 27:30

"And concerning the tithe of the herd or the flock, of whatever passes under the rod, the tenth one shall be holy to the Lord." Leviticus 27:32

What is clear is that the tithe came from crops and flocks or herds. The ones who gave the tithe were the landowners. Those who worked the land did not have to pay a tithe. Those who made and sold things did not pay a tithe on the money they made from the sale.

A carpenter did not pay a tithe unless he grew his own crops (such as mint and cumin) and then he paid a tithe on the crops, not the money received from selling the objects he made or from the work he did.

The tithe came from the increase, not the income.

The tithe clearly took the form of the crops (and crop produce such as wine or oil) and animals that had been produced on the land. Deuteronomy 12 explains that it was the landowner's responsibility to pay the tithe on behalf of his whole household, his sons and

daughters, menservants and maidservants and the
Levites from their towns.

Rabbi Dr Louis Jacobs asserts that

> *"according the Rabbis, the laws of tithing*
> *only apply to the land of Israel, and farmers*
> *in the Diaspora have no obligation to give*
> *tithes..."* (Jacobs)

This means that those who had to pay a tithe were the
landowners/farmers but only if they lived in Israel.

How many tithes?

The farmers were required to give three kinds of tithes.
The first of the three kinds of tithe was the Levitical
tithe (as outlined in Numbers 18:21 – 24). This tithe
was given on what remained after the heave offering
had been given. It was given to the Levites and the
Levites were required to give a tenth (or a tithe) of the
tithe to the Priests (this was actually not considered a
tithe, but a heave offering as well, according to
Numbers 18:28).

The Priests were also funded and supported by the
heave offerings, all the holy gifts of the children of
Israel (Numbers 18:8 – 20). They were considered

holy and no-one except the Priests and their families, not even the Levites, were allowed to eat it or they would die (Numbers 18:32).

Such holy gifts included sin offerings, trespass offerings, grain and wave offerings, first fruit offerings and the offerings of everything that first opens the womb. The heave offering had no set amount and was given at the farmer's discretion however, Rabbi Louis Jacobs says that it was around a sixtieth, fiftieth or fortieth.

There are some people who teach that even if a person doesn't tithe, then they should give offerings and the minimum offering should be ten percent. Most offerings in the Bible were voluntary and there was no minimum set.

The tithe was a form of taxation system. The offerings, in particular, the heave offering, were actually tax deductions or salary sacrifices. The more heave offering a farmer gave, the less tithe he paid. He paid his tithe as a percentage of what he had left after his offering.

Our society is not set up that way. Generally, governments don't allow us to use offerings as a salary sacrifice or tax deduction. In most cases tax is taken out of our wage first and we give tithes and offerings out of what's left (some based on the pre-tax amount and some on the after-tax amount). Again, it is the opposite of what's in the Bible.

Tithe 1

The purpose of this first tithe was to provide for the Levites (Refer to Numbers 18:21-24). They were given no inheritance and they were not allowed to work outside of the tabernacle of meeting. The tabernacle of meeting eventually became the temple.

The role of the Levite was to attend to the needs of the Priest and the tabernacle. The Levites could not come near the sanctuary or the altar or they would die. The Priests could not own land and they were not allowed to work for their own money. Their sole purpose was to carry out the work of the sanctuary and the altar, daily offering sacrifices to God on behalf of themselves, the people and the nation of Israel as a whole.

The Priests and the Levites had no other way of supporting themselves or their families. In return for their work, God allowed them to live off the tithes and offerings that were brought in by the people. They had nothing they could leave their children. God Himself was their portion and their inheritance (Numbers 18:20).

To bring this into modern terms in a way things are sometimes compared, the Pastors (the Priests) of the temple/tabernacle (church) received the offerings. The worship team, the cleaners, the maintenance people, the kitchen staff etc., (the Levites) received the tithes.

Most of the Levitical roles that can be compared to activities in modern churches are carried out by volunteers. The tithes and offerings are often combined to pay the pastors wages and building maintenance. There are a number of churches that run other programs and those programs are sometimes required to be self-funding or need special offerings.

Tithe 2

The second tithe described was the Feast Tithe. The primary reference for this is Deuteronomy 14:22-23. Verses 24 to 27 outline what to do if the journey to the place to where God has chosen to make His name abide is too long. Deuteronomy 12:6-7 also describe the second tithe.

The idea is that a tenth (a tithe) of the increase of the grain, the wine, the oil and the firstborn are brought to the place chosen by God and there, His blessing is celebrated by feasting on the outcome of His blessing. In other words, the tither is meant to eat and drink the tithe.

The tither is again encouraged not to forget the Levite as he has no part or inheritance with the children of Israel.

Tithe 3

The third tithe is the Poor Tithe. This is recorded in Deuteronomy 14:28. Every third and sixth year (the seventh year is the Sabbath year, no crops were harvested and therefore no tithes were given) the tithe was set aside and stored up to feed the Levite, the widow, the fatherless and the stranger in the land.

There is much debate about whether the tithe system was really one tithe distributed different ways (10%), two tithes, with the second used in two different ways (20%) or three different tithes, one of them only given every three years (23 1/3%).

Rabbinic literature describes the following system. The *Terumah* (the heave offering) was removed from the yield first and given to a Priest. This was a portion of the yield and the amount was determined by the farmer.

A tenth of the remainder, known as *ma'aser rishon* (the first tithe), was given to the Levite, who then gives a tenth of that to the Priest.

The farmer then separates another tenth of the remainder called *ma'aser sheni* (the second tithe), takes it to Jerusalem and feasts on it (remembering to give some to the Levite).

Every third and sixth year the second tithe is given to the poor. It is known as *ma'aser ani* (the poor man's tithe). (Jacobs)

This indicates that the tithing system as set up under The Law, was in fact 20% of the increase in the produce of the land, given after the harvest. Of that 20%, half was to be consumed by the tither to recognise God's goodness (except for the third and sixth year, when it was stored up for the poor).

The other half was given to the Levites as compensation for having no inheritance and not being able to work.

Any time we read about the tithe from Exodus until after the death of Jesus, we need to put it into the context of the 20% for the purposes of supporting the Levites (who were not allowed to earn their own money), celebrating the goodness of God and providing for the poor. It is also only relating to farmers living in Israel and is the produce from the land, not cash.

Some people may say that today's society does not have the same agricultural emphasis as did ancient Israel, that cash was uncommon then, so what was agricultural should be changed to money. However, money was definitely used at the time the tithing system was set up.

There were people who worked the land and were paid by the landholders. There were people who had other occupations that did not involve working the land. There were blacksmiths, carpenters, potters and tailors to name a few. None of those were required to pay tithes.

Why just the farmers?

What was significant about the produce of the land? *I believe* it was because the farmers back then were at the mercy of the environment. They didn't irrigate their crops, they didn't have antibiotics and they couldn't genetically modify plants to make them disease resistant.

The farmers had to totally rely on God's blessing and His goodness to receive any increase. It wasn't really based on their skills or gifting as farmers (although they still needed to be diligent).

If God didn't look after them they wouldn't have an increase. That meant when they gave a tithe, they gave it completely based on God's blessing, not on a mix of what they achieved through their skills, gifting or the work of their hands *and* God's provision.

One time when money is mentioned with tithing is in the Deuteronomy 14 passage. This is in particular reference to the Feast Tithe. Here it says that if the chosen place is too far then the tither can sell the goods he was going to tithe, take the money to the chosen place, buy whatever their heart desires to eat or drink, then eat, drink and rejoice.

This is the one time when **income** could be related to the tithe. In this case though, the tithe is not 10% of the income derived from the sale of the produce. It is 100% of the sale of 10% of the increase in produce. There is a difference.

The tithe was given on the increase that could be directly attributed to God. It was not given on the income derived from the increase. If it was on the income, the farmer could choose to accumulate and store the produce and therefore not tithe anything.

The farmer could also claim that the income resulted from his ability to negotiate a price or trade for the produce and could say that he tithed more based on his skill and not on God's blessing. If the tithe was based on the income derived from the sale of the produce, it would be affected by fluctuations in the value of the goods. Again, the amount is the result of man and not God.

The tithe, as described under the Law was to be given based on **increase** that resulted from God's blessing. It was not to be given on the income that resulted from man's efforts.

The other time when money is mentioned, is when the tither wants to buy back the tithe he has given. In this case he is able to purchase the tithe for an extra one fifth of its value. This is equivalent to paying 12% if you wanted to pay money instead of giving the tithe of the produce.

Here the farmer is not tithing on income. He is the one paying. He buys back the increase he was supposed to have tithed. I believe that one reason the value was increased was so the farmer would not generate income from what was supposed to be a tithe.

The tithe was not associated with income, instead it was based on increase as provided by God.

Offerings

The offerings were given for a variety of reasons. Some were compulsory, some were voluntary, some were specific in amounts and items and others were up to the farmer's discretion.

Some offerings were sacrifices for sin, others were given simply as a free will gift and still others were purchased back from the Priest. All offerings were produce from the land, were the best of the produce (unlike tithes) and served a dual purpose.

The offering was given exclusively to God (whether as a sacrifice for sin or a gift) and the Priest was given permission to eat or drink it. The offering was holy and only the Priest or his family could eat it.

This permission to consume the offering was given to compensate the Priest for the fact that he had no inheritance, no land and no income. The tithe was given to the Levite. The offering was given to God who then gave it to the Priest.

It should also be noted that the only way the priest was able to receive the offering was because of the offerings he made for himself. There were purification rites that the Priest had to go through in order to be able to receive the offerings. These purification rites are no longer in operation and so these offerings are no longer given.

No more tithing under the law

The temple no longer stands, therefore there is no need to bring in the tithes as there is no Levitical or Priestly order to provide for. Hebrews chapter 7 explains that there has been a change in the Priestly order. It is no longer the Levitical order. The new Priest is a Priest forever according to the order of Melchizedek.

Jesus, our High Priest, does not need to offer sacrifices for us or Himself. He made one Sacrifice, for all. Since the temple is either in Heaven being readied to come down with the New Jerusalem, or is our own bodies, there's no need for the Levites to take care of it. There is no requirement to bring in tithes or offerings.

For the most part, Jews who live in Israel today, do not tithe as is outlined according to these scriptures. In fact to do so would be unlawful.

Rabbi Eliezer Melamid speaks of the *ma'aser k'safim* (*maser kesafim*, according to Rabbi Dr. Louis Jacobs). This is known as 'the money tithe' or 'wealth tax.' It is a custom that numerous observant Jews participate in and involves giving 10% of their annual income to charity.

Some may say that this practise is the same as what we know as the modern version of tithing. Here are some significant differences. This tithe does not go to a temple, synagogue, Priest, Levite or even Rabbi. It must go to a recognised charity. Rabbi Eliezer Melamid spoke against the practice of using that tithe even for the purposes of preparing the *bar* or *bat mitzvah*.

The bar or bat mitzvah is the 13 year old boy or 12 year old girl who is prepared to take an active role in society. People often suppose that the bar mitzvah is the ceremony, but that's not the case. Preparing the bar or bat mitzvah involves paying for tutors for the boy or girl to learn Hebrew, being sent to special Jewish schools and other places to learn the Law and being active in community, charitable activities.

In Western culture, if the children receive that kind of preparation, it usually comes from the church. Rabbi Eliezer Melamid specifically says that the tithe should **not** go the institutions who provide this kind of preparation.

This tithe is not to be used for religious education (there is however some discussion amongst Jewish scholars about the validity of that stand). The poor are not meant to pay this tithe. Rabbi Eliezer Melamid states in his writings that if you are using your money wisely and you put your *ma'aser k'safin* in to a charity but lack the funds to pay for the religious education for your children, you are too poor to pay the money tithe. Pay for your children's education instead. (Melamid 2014)

What about other giving?

Not all the giving done in Israel was under the context of the tithe/tax system. We can see a number of examples of incredible generosity and I'd like to look at two of them. Both of these examples involved the construction of dwelling places for the presence of God.

The first example of this generosity is seen in Exodus 35 – 36 when Moses asks the people for an offering for the construction of the Tabernacle. The offering came from those who had a willing heart.

Those who gave were the ones whose hearts were stirred and whose spirits were willing. They brought the Lord's offering. In fact, so much was brought as offerings that people had to be restrained from bringing more.

In this instance of extravagant giving, there was no obligation. The people freely brought their offerings with willing hearts overflowing with joy and excitement in being able to contribute to the place containing the presence of God. They were moved by God and their own spirits to give. Giving to a vision can stimulate giving with joy and enthusiasm.

As yet, I haven't seen our congregation so inspired that I have to send deacons out to intercept people before they put more money into an offering bag. I'm thinking of buying extra offering bags for just that occasion though.

The second instance I would like to look at is David's gifts to the construction of the temple. We find this recorded in 1 Chronicles 29.

David, in his devotion to God, not only gives the resources of his kingdom, but also resources from his personal treasury. David asked the other leaders if they would contribute and the Bible says they gave willingly.

> *"The people rejoiced at the willing response of their leaders, for they had given freely and wholeheartedly to the Lord." 1 Chronicles 29:9*

Again, there was no obligation. This was a free will offering. Between David and his leaders they gave personal offerings of gold and silver equivalent to $6,300,000,000 USD.

The above figure is based on gold's value being $38 USD per gram and silver being $0.51 USD per gram. It is also using the measure of a talent to be 20kg. The measure of a talent could be anywhere between 20kg and 40kg at that time. This figure did not include the value of the bronze, iron and precious stones that were also given.

The kind of giving that inspired rejoicing was free will, wholehearted, Holy Spirit inspired giving. This kind of giving comes freely from the inside out, not imposed from the outside in.

It may also be important to note that while I would love to use these scriptures to *inspire* people to give to a building fund, I would over-step my authority to say that those scriptures tell us we *should* give to a building fund. Both cases are examples of free will offerings bringing joy. There is no obligation in them. Obligation brings bondage.

Also, the only temples today that house the presence of God are our bodies. I'm not sure if 'Gym Membership' and 'Protein Shake Program' are what people have in mind when I speak about raising money to build 'The House of God.' I can't imagine anyone except my wife seeing that as a vision that would inspire extravagant, free will, joyous giving.

To sum up

- People under the Law generally gave in the form of tithes and offerings. The tithes were a requirement as were some of the offerings. Other offerings were completely free will.

- The tithes were a set figure of 20% of the increase of crops and flocks, or 22% if you were going to pay cash in place of one of the tithes.

- People seemed to give most joyously when they gave freely and not out of obligation (Free will offerings, not tithing).

- They were supposed to eat and drink 10% of the tithe to celebrate God's goodness.

- Any reference to tithing in the Bible, from Exodus to Revelation is referring to tithing under the Law.

- The tithe was based on increase, not income.

- The modern day concept of the tithe is completely different to any tithe outlined in the Bible.

- Tithing under the Law and in Jewish culture helped provide for those who did not have a good source of income. The tithe was never required of those who didn't have a good source of income. This included the Priests and Levites who were *not allowed* to work (apart from Temple or Tabernacle responsibilities) for an income.

- Today, according to the Law, tithes should not be paid.

According to the Law, you are free from any obligation to give tithes and offerings. Obligation Free! I don't know about you, but I get happy thinking about that. I still want to give, because it's become part of my character, but I love the fact that I don't *have* to. I'm free and that fills me with joy.

Chapter 4: There's Robbing And Cursing And Tithing. Oh Malachi!

The Yellow Brick Road

Sometimes my experiences with tithes and offerings have left me feeling like Dorothy in the Land of Oz. Dorothy wanted to get home and the Wizard of Oz promised to help, but only after she had carried out certain tasks. She faced many threats, fears and obstacles both getting to the wizard and carrying out the Wizard's tasks in order to get his help. A phrase that comes to mind is 'jumping through hoops.'

After Dorothy had jumped through all the hoops, she got back to the Wizard and found out that he was a fraud. His seemingly all powerful, supernatural powers were just smoke and mirrors. He got what he wanted by tricking people, bullying them and manipulating them. This is the Wizard, not God and not preachers.

In the movie 'The Wizard of Oz,' Dorothy found that even her journey to the Wizard was dangerous, because on the Yellow Brick Road, 'There's lions and tigers and bears. Oh my!'

I don't know if other people have felt like this, but the journey to the blessing of God through tithes and offerings has felt to me like a series of hoops that need to be jumped through. There's tasks that need to be completed if I am to access the promises of God. The problem is that when I've completed them, the promises, at times, aren't fulfilled.

The journey to the blessing of God can seem quite dangerous, because according to Malachi, there's robbing and cursing and tithing. Oh my!

The above statements have been my *perception*, not the truth. There's a big difference. They are the result of my lack of understanding and faith, holding on to false expectations and misperceptions of the character of God.

Malachi 3:8-10

"Will a man rob God? Yet you have robbed me!

But you say, 'In what way have we robbed You?'

In tithes and offerings.

You are cursed with a curse, for you have robbed Me, even this whole nation.

Bring all the tithes into the storehouse, that there may be food in My house and try Me now in this," says the Lord of Hosts, "If I will not open for you the windows of heaven and pour out for you such blessing that there will not be room enough to receive it."

Scary and exciting

This scripture is used extensively to support the paying of tithes and offerings. And honestly, who would not want to give tithes and offerings after reading this? Robbing God, cursed with a curse, overflowing blessings if they are paid?

The way this passage has been explained to me in the past, is that if I don't give my tithes and offerings I am robbing God. If I rob God, I'll be cursed. If I give my tithes and offerings I will be blessed and blessed to overflowing. As a Christian, I don't want to rob God. I don't want to be cursed. I want God's blessing.

We are sometimes further taught that tithes on their own won't do it. Tithes will open the windows of heaven, but it is only offerings that cause the blessings to be poured out. If we don't pay tithes, the windows don't open, so the tithe has to be paid first. Offerings made above the tithe will cause the blessings to flow. The promise is that we can test God and see if He won't do what He promises.

That gets me excited and scared at the same time. I'm excited because of the promise and I'm scared because of the threat.

What was the setting?

Malachi was considered a prophet, bringing a word from God. He addressed a number of issues including corruption in the religious order. The book is placed at a time after the Israelites had returned from exile in Persia and after the temple had been rebuilt.

He may have been working at a similar time as Ezra and Nehemiah. Haggai and Zechariah were also around at a similar time. What is interesting is that both Nehemiah and Malachi address the issue of a corrupt priesthood and the payment of tithes.

Nehemiah (Nehemiah 13) came to Jerusalem to take charge of the rebuilding of the walls and to re-establish leadership for the people. He returned to Persia for a period of time and when he came back he found that corruption had entered the priesthood.

The person in charge of the storehouse had emptied the large room and given that room to the Tobia the Ammonite. The priesthood was disregarding the Law and many were giving laws to profit themselves instead of helping the people.

Nehemiah dealt with the evil of the Ammonite, and the keeper of the storehouse but found that the Levites were unable to carry out their function in the temple as they were out working in the fields. This was for two reasons. They were not being given their portion of the tithe, and the people had stopped bringing in their tithes and offerings because of the corruption in the temple.

When the people saw that Nehemiah was dealing with the corruption, they began to bring the tithes back to the storehouses.

Malachi was written at a time when the priests were corrupt, the Levites were working in the field and the people were withholding their tithes.

In Malachi chapter 1, the author, on behalf of God, addresses the polluted offerings that are being brought by the people. Even if the offerings were pure, the priests who sacrificed them were not and so the offering was unacceptable to God.

Malachi chapter 2 addresses the issue of corrupt priests and the infidelity of the people. In Malachi chapter 3, the coming Messenger is prophesied and the ones that judgement is coming against are mentioned. These included the sorcerers, adulterers, perjurers and **those who exploit wage earners, widows and orphans and those who turn away an alien**. After that, tithes and offerings are mentioned.

So this is the context of the scripture written at the beginning of this chapter. The priesthood was corrupt, the Levites were out working in the fields, worshippers of other gods were doing business in the temple courts on the Sabbath, the men were unfaithful to their wives, the poor were being oppressed, the people had given up bringing in their tithes and any sacrifices that were made were ineffectual and therefore the nation remained covered in its sin.

The Curse

Deuteronomy 30 makes it clear that when the Law was established, the Israelites were given the choice of being blessed or cursed. If they kept all the Law they would have blessing. If they didn't keep the Law but they had appropriate sacrifices, they would have blessing. If they didn't keep the Law and they didn't have the appropriate sacrifices they would end up under a curse.

If we look at the curse in Malachi we can see that the curse the people of Israel were cursed with was because they were not keeping the whole of the law.

Often people attribute the statement of being cursed with not paying the tithe. It says, "You are cursed with a curse, for you have robbed Me, even this whole nation."

It appears from that line that cursing is directly attributed to not tithing. If we look at Deuteronomy 27 though, we see the list of things that the people were going to be cursed for under the Law.

58

> *"Cursed is the one who perverts the justice due the stranger, the fatherless and the widow." Deuteronomy 27:19*

According to Brown-Driver-Briggs this passage could be interpreted "Cursed is the one who thrusts aside the legal rights and privileges due to those in need." (Brown, Driver, Briggs 2006)

Those in need had a legal right to be fed from the storehouse where the tithes were kept. To withhold that legal right was to come under a curse. Deuteronomy 27:26 adds to that and says that anyone who doesn't observe the Law will come under a curse. So when this is examined we see that the curse came as a result of breaking the Law, not directly by not paying tithes.

Cookie eating

When I was younger my dad baked some cookies. He put them on a bench and told me not to touch them. They were yummy looking cookies and I was sure they wanted to be eaten, after all, that's what they were created for. But I wasn't allowed to touch them.

One of the cookies was evil though, and it told me that if I shoved the cookie over to the edge of the bench with a fork and ate it from the bench, then I wouldn't be touching it.

When my father came back in the room and found that I had eaten a cookie, he punished me for my disobedience. I told him that I hadn't touched the cookie, that I'd used a fork. He said that I must have touched it with my mouth when I ate it. It showed me that while a cookie might be evil, it's not an evil genius and certainly not as smart as my father.

After tea that evening Dad handed around the plate of cookies. He passed it to me first, but I wasn't falling for it. No way was I going to touch those cookies. They were bad news. Dad explained to me that I could eat the cookies now. It had been the wrong time to eat them earlier. Now was the right time.

Apparently it wasn't the cookie eating that was the trouble, it was the cookie eating at the wrong time that was not allowed. Cookie eating was OK in the right circumstances but cookie eating was also not OK in the wrong circumstances.

This is the same as tithing. Not tithing in itself was not the problem, because there were many circumstances in which tithing was not done (such as living outside Israel, not being a farmer, being poor and every seventh year). It was the circumstances surrounding not tithing that meant the Law was broken and *that* made not tithing a problem.

The curse came from what the lack of tithing caused

We see this validated by the passages Malachi 3:5 and 7. Verse 5 speaks of those who will be judged, including those who exploit wage earners, widows and orphans and mistreat aliens (Deuteronomy 27:19). Verse 7 tells the Israelites that they continue to turn away from the Law (Ordinances) and that God wants them to turn back.

The people ask how and God answers them with Malachi 3:8-10. Bring in the tithes and the offerings. The offerings and sacrifices can be made so the people's sin is washed away and they can step out from under the curse. The storehouse can be made full so those in need can be provided for. The Levites can be supplied with their food so they can continue to serve the way they are meant to.

Can we be cursed?

So in looking at this information, can we come under a curse if we do not pay tithes? The answer to that is yes … if we live under the Law and if we live in Israel and if we are farmers and if there is a temple to bring the offerings to and if there is a storehouse to bring the tithe to, and if there is a Priestly and Levitical order in effective operation requiring our support because they are not allowed to provide for themselves in any other way.

If every single one of the circumstances just mentioned applies to us then we will come under a curse if we don't pay the tithes. If however, even one of those circumstances does not apply to us then we are not breaking the Law and we will not come under a curse.

Robbing God

Malachi 3:8-10 is addressed to the Israelites who lived in Israel. Can *we* rob God by not bringing in the tithes and the offerings if we live outside of Israel? The answer to that is no.

This passage refers to the legal requirements of tithes and offerings as set out through Exodus to Deuteronomy. We do not live under the Law and there is no requirement for us to bring in tithes and offerings.

Cookies again

If I went to a shop that offered free cookie samples, would I be robbing the shop if I took a free sample? No.

If the shop owners said that all donations were gratefully accepted if I eat a cookie sample, would I be robbing them if I didn't pay? No.

If they said that a donation *was* required and I didn't give them a donation then I *would* be robbing the shop. Tithing here is the same.

If there is no legal requirement to pay tithes and offerings, and I don't pay them, I'm not robbing God. If paying tithes and offerings is a good idea and I don't pay them, then I'm not robbing God. If tithes and offerings are a requirement and I don't pay them, *then* I'm robbing God.

You're not robbing God

The requirement makes it a law. Have you been told that you are not under Law, but if you don't pay tithes then you're robbing God? If you have, then Law was being imposed on you. How can it be robbery if you don't pay something you are not required to pay?

Even if we lived under the Law, we would still not be robbing God if we didn't pay the tithes. The reason for that is that most people who read this will be living outside of Israel and don't grow crops or have flocks or herds and according to the Law these are the conditions for paying the tithes.

What if you had crops, flocks or herds and you lived in Israel? The answer is still no. There is no temple to bring the tithes and offerings to. The Priests or Levites who are around, do not receive tithes and do not make offerings on your behalf (because there's no temple). And, according to Hebrews, there's a new Priestly order anyway. You are **not** robbing God if you do not pay your tithes and offerings.

All The Tithes

When discussing tithing with people, a number of times I have had people tell me that they feel confident in being able to receive God's blessings because they bring in all their tithes to the storehouse.

They have no doubts that God will provide for them because they have been faithful to give all the tithe and an offering and God said to test Him in that and see if He doesn't bless as He promised. It's in the Bible.

Sometimes I ask if they always bring their 10% to the church. They say they do, plus extra for the offering. Then I ask if they bring it in cash or produce.

They tell me that they bring it in cash of course, plus the offering so the blessing will pour out of the window that was opened by the tithe, and they bring it to church because the church is the modern version of the temple and the storehouse.

I then tell them that if they want Malachi 3 to apply to them then they have to bring all the tithe and offerings to the storehouse. They say they do. I ask them if it is all 20% or 22% if they have a cash component, and that's not counting the offerings. They say "What?"

I then explain that this passage refers to tithing as applied to the children of Israel under the Law. I outline the tithes that were required, the 10% of their produce for their feast and the 10% of the produce for the storehouse (plus the extra 20% of the 10% if they wanted to keep the produce and pay cash). And then there were the offerings that were meant to be given before the tithe.

Unfortunately, a person can't claim the promises and blessings that come with the keeping of the Law if they don't keep the whole Law.

> 'And I testify again to every man who becomes circumcised that he is a debtor to keep the whole law.' Galatians 5:3

The implication here is that if you aim to keep one part of the Law in order to receive the blessing, or for whatever reason, you are then required to keep the whole of the Law.

Paul uses the idea of circumcision in this instance because that is what the Galatians were being told they had to do. The point is valid though for any aspect of the Law.

> 'For whoever shall keep the whole law, and yet stumble in one point, he is guilty of all.' James 2:10

These two passages very clearly tell us that we cannot keep one part of the Law only and dismiss the rest. If we try to keep one part of it, we need to keep the rest. If we fail in the keeping of one part of the Law, we fail in it all.

If I try to keep the tithing aspect of the Law, then I also have to keep the not eating bacon side of the Law. If I eat bacon then regardless of how well I kept tithing, I have failed in that as well.

It also means that unless I bring the *whole* tithe and the offerings, as outlined according to the Law, into the storehouse I will not receive the blessing. If I attempt to keep that part of the Law, for whatever reason, I will need to keep the whole of the Law and if I fail in any part of the Law I fail in it all.

If I fail in the Law, I will come under a curse. When living under the Law, the only way around the curse, the only way to enter the blessing, is to offer the appropriate sacrifices, as outlined by the Law.

The question to ask when aiming for the blessing of Malachi 3 based on your tithes is 'Am I really paying *all* the tithe and am I trying to claim the blessing that comes with paying *all* the tithe?'

The Blessing

There are many people, who, with good intentions, teach and practice the tithing concept and try to claim the promises of Malachi 3. Because they do not carry out tithing according to the stipulations of the Law, however, they will never enter into the blessing promised by that scripture, **if they rely solely on their own merits**.

I have seen people blessed, not because they religiously adhere to the type of tithing taught today, but because God honours faith. These people don't rely on the tithe to bring the blessing, even though they give it. They rely on the One who made the promise, to keep His promise.

God looks at people's hearts and He sees their intentions and in His grace He overlooks their failure to keep the Law correctly and blesses them in spite of themselves.

People who have tithed all their lives may read this book and have resentment and bitterness rise up. They may begin to question the worth of what they have done. I would like to honour them for their faithfulness. They have been faithful to give as they were taught and God honours that too.

The giving they did was in faith and it has not gone to waste.

I once heard a minister tell his story of one of his experiences. He was calling people forward for healing. He was on a stage and an elderly lady with a walker approached the stage.

The minister thought it would be spectacular to jump off the stage and land right in front of the lady, laying his hand on her head and shouting 'Be healed.' He judged his jump and leapt. The only problem was that just as he jumped, the elderly lady took an extra-large step and stood right where the minister was about to land.

He crashed into her and they rolled on the floor until he was lying on his back and she was lying over the top of him. He thought he was going to have to deal with a lawsuit. The lady pushed herself off him, jumped in the air shouting that she was healed and then ran around the auditorium to prove it.

The point here is that no matter what we do, if we do it in faith, God will use it to do something amazing. If you are one of the ones who have tithed faithfully and are beginning to see something different, don't be discouraged. Know with absolute assurance that God has taken what you have given, is pouring His blessing over you and using your giving to show His glory.

One thing I find interesting is that nearly all of the references the Apostle Paul makes to the promises of blessings are references to promises made before the Law was introduced. They usually point to the promises given to Abraham.

As was mentioned earlier, those promises of blessings were fulfilled (apart from the promise of an heir) before Abraham tithed.

> *'For all the promises of God in Him (Jesus) are yes, and in Him (Jesus) amen, to the glory of God through us.' 2 Corinthians 1:20*

The fulfilment of promises comes as a result of the finished work of Jesus at the cross, through grace and faith given to us by God. Our being able to receive the promises is dependent on faith not on our fulfillment of the Law.

> *'And if you are Christ's, then you are Abraham's seed and heirs according to the promise.' Galatians 3:29*

This is the reason we are able to receive blessings. We *inherit* the blessing, through faith. We don't earn it by keeping the Law.

Did you get that? You receive the blessing of God because of your family relationship not your effort. How good is that? That has to bring a bit of joy in.

There are many promises of blessings after the introduction of the Law and they are dependent on fulfilling the obligations of the Law. Thankfully, Jesus did fulfil the Law on our behalf and so we are able to receive the blessings associated with the Law apart from the Law. Even if very few of these blessings are referred to after the death of Jesus the Bible tells us that *all* the promises of God are yes and amen.

Let's look at the blessing that is promised in Malachi 3.

Heaven's windows

The first part of the blessing speaks of God opening up the windows of heaven and pouring out a blessing. What comes out of the windows of heaven?

The only time the "windows of heaven" are mentioned apart from Malachi is in relation to rain, the rain of the flood. There is a reference to the doors of heaven and out of those came manna and quail, but the windows of heaven only refer to rain.

There is also a reference in 2 Kings 7 to the windows *in* heaven. The context of this is actually comparing the abundance of grain to the abundance of rain at the time of the flood. Today, when we speak of the heavens opening it is usually in context of a deluge of rain.

Now I know that we live in New Testament times and so things that happened in the natural are shadows of

71

the spiritual. What does the New Testament say about the windows of heaven? Nothing.

There is mention of heaven opening. In those times, people saw into heaven. They had a vision. What came out of the open heaven?

One time there was the Holy Spirit in the form of a dove, another time, associated with a vision was a blanket covered with unclean animals and another time it was Christ on a white horse riding out to war. There is no mention of heaven opening and having financial blessing poured out over us.

This blessing in Malachi is actually speaking about rain. It is rain to water the crops and give good ground coverage for the flocks and herds to eat. The purpose of it is so that the storehouses will be full to feed those in need. A side benefit is that the farmer's barns are full as well.

So we *will* be blessed if we tithe? Have you ever noticed that the more intimate you are with God, the higher expectation He has of you? Some of the things you got away with as a baby Christian, God doesn't let you get away with as a more mature Christian. Have you ever noticed that behaviours or attitudes God challenges you on He doesn't challenge others on?

This situation is a bit like this. God was withholding His blessing to get the attention of His people. Others were getting away with the same behaviour, but blessing wasn't being held back from them. God loves people and He blesses them because it is His nature.

Sometimes He withholds blessing because:

> *"For whom the Lord loves, He chastens."*
> *(Hebrews 12:6).*

To receive the blessing of God doesn't mean you're a good or righteous person, it just means you're a person. Jesus says that the Father:

> *"...causes His sun to rise on the evil and the good, and sends rain (blessing, according to Malachi 3) on the righteous and the unrighteous." Matthew 5:45*

There is a teaching that if a person faithfully gives their tithes the windows of heaven will open. The teaching says that giving offerings will cause the blessings to pour out. These are the hoops to jump through.

If only an offering is given then the windows of heaven remain closed. If only a tithe is given, the blessing remains inaccessible on the other side of the open window. God is not going to release the blessing until the offering is given.

The truth is that being blessed has very little to do with us. The only thing we have to do with being blessed is to receive it. A lot of Christians don't receive blessing because they feel so bad about themselves through shame and condemnation, they believe they don't deserve it.

If God blesses the unrighteous, why wouldn't he bless those who are made righteous by the blood of His beloved Son? Do we deserve it? No, but He blesses us anyway. He is the Father.

God is the Father

Our blessing is not dependent on what we do to earn it, the works we do or what we give. It is dependent on the faith we have to receive them from a loving Father whose heart is for us. If you have children, think about your relationship with them.

Do you provide the best environment you can for your children, for growth, physically, mentally, emotionally and spiritually based on their behaviour or how much they do for you? Or do you do it because they are your children? If we are made in God's image, if we are a reflection of Him, then surely His desire to bless His children simply because He loves them would be greater than our own.

A good year

So what about the other parts of the blessing? If we pay our tithes and our offerings, it says that God will rebuke the devourer, the fruit of our ground will not be destroyed and the vines will not fail to bear fruit.

If we look at all this in the context of Malachi 3 what we see is God reaffirming the promises He made if they kept all the Law. If they paid the tithes, if they gave the appropriate offerings and made the right sacrifices, God would provide the right environment for their crops and herds to prosper.

God would provide the right amount of rain (opening up the windows of heaven), He would make good soil, He would provide the right amount of warmth and He would keep away the locusts and the fungi that rot the plants. He wanted the tithe to come from the work of His hands, not ours.

If we look at wine growing, apparently, the very best wines are the ones, not produced by the best wine maker, but in the best location. The right grape needs to be matched to the right climate. This leaves the wine industry at the mercy of nature.

A good year for a wine is one where the climate perfectly matches the requirements of the grapevine. A bad year occurs when, no matter what the vine dresser does or how good he is, the weather does not suit the needs of the grapevine and the quality of grape produced, just does not make wine as good as in other years.

A good year is a good year, a bad year is a bad year and there's nothing that can be done about it. The only thing to do is to roll with the punches.

God's promise of blessing in Malachi is for a good year, every year. It will be that He provides the right environment required for fruitful living. He will cause the windows of heaven to open so the right amount of rain or sunlight shines through.

He will provide the right amount of warmth and the right kind of soil. He will protect the fruit from the things which would consume or spoil it.

> *'Blessed be the God and Father of our Lord Jesus Christ, who has blessed us with every spiritual blessing in the heavenly places in Christ.' Ephesians 1:3*

We are blessed with *every* spiritual blessing. Every spiritual blessing includes having a good year. This is not because of us keeping all of the Law, it is because of what Jesus Christ did for us at the cross. It is by *His* work that we are blessed.

The Storehouse

Malachi tells the Jewish people to bring the tithes into the storehouse, that there might be food in God's house. This means that the Jewish nation was to bring food (the tithe) into the place where the food was stored (the storehouse), so the Levites, the widows, the orphans and the strangers in the land would have food to eat when they needed it.

There would be food at the temple (God's house). This met the needs of the Levites who had no other source of income, and were not allowed to have any (or were not meant to anyway).

It was also a practical demonstration of love for other people who were less fortunate than those who brought the tithes into the storehouse. The widow, the orphan and the stranger in the land had, at times, very little opportunity to support themselves and so would need help with food.

Modern teaching says that we should bring money (tithes) to the church (the storehouse) so there will be food (sermons, spiritual food) in the church (temple, aka God's house).

There are a number of problems with interpreting this passage from Malachi in this way. The first problem is with the definition of what a tithe is. Remember that the tithe in Malachi is the tithe as described under the Law. It is not **the regular giving of ten percent of a person's income, no matter what the source.**

The second problem is the purpose of the tithe. In Malachi the purpose was to receive food from rich people and give it to people who were unable to obtain it by their own means.

These days, the tithe comes from every socio-economic status to keep the 'church' running and pay for the staff. Some money is then put in to community projects, however the primary focus is the running of the 'church' organisation.

At times people who are poor are compelled to give even when it costs them meals to do it. The very system that was set up to help provide for these people is used to take from them.

Faith without works is dead

This third problem is related to the second. James 2 speaks of faith without works being dead. In verses 15 and 16 of chapter 2 he suggests an example of a person being without food or clothing.

James then asks what good is it if someone speaks in faith for the person to be warmed and filled but doesn't help them get clothes or food. The person provides for a spiritual need but does nothing to meet the physical needs of the body.

We can look at that and think, 'Well of course we should help them. How ridiculous! Why would someone pray but do nothing of practical value?' When we look at it though, this is exactly what we do in churches with the tithe.

Rich and poor are, in some congregations, compelled to bring money into the 'church' organisation even at the cost of poor people missing out on food and being able to replace clothes. They are then told that the food they receive is spiritual food.

Yes a spiritual need is met, however the physical need is not only not met, but even exacerbated. This is dead faith. It is the very thing James speaks against.

As a side note, I believe there is another part to the message on faith that James brings. I believe that James is saying we shouldn't project our revelation of faith in God as provider onto someone in need.

What we should do is meet that person's need (as directed by God) and live in our revelation and faith of God as provider. Perhaps the reason we don't give at times is because we don't really have that revelation and we are afraid we will be in need if we give.

As a pastor, I see it worked out in the congregation this way. I need to get a good revelation of God as provider so I will have faith in *God's* provision when I am in a place of seeming lack. In this place I can be a blessing to others despite the figures on my bank balance.

The faith I have can be an inspiration to others, not an expectation on them. It means that when financial pressure is on me, it's not passed on to the congregation.

I don't project my faith on to the congregation and then put pressure on them to give regardless of their financial position. I believe God for His provision and the congregation can draw off that for their provision.

The church is not a building

The fourth problem is that the church building is not a storehouse. It is not a temple and it is not the house of God. It is a building. The church is the people, it is the body of Christ. People don't go to church, they are the church.

Our bodies are the temple, we are living stones and we are God's house. We are the storehouse of God's love, His presence and His Word. We are to give freely of what God has deposited in us to those who are around us. Our actions and our words should demonstrate the charity of God towards those He loves.

This will happen, not because we work at it, but because we are transformed into the image of Christ by the power of the Holy Spirit. As we become more like Him, as we take on His character and nature, we will naturally do the things He does. This change occurs through intimacy with God and surrender to His Holy Spirit.

Sin offerings are finished

Something else to consider with the Malachi passage, is the argument that pastors have now taken over the role of the Priest and the Levite, and so they need the tithes and offerings coming in to support them financially. It is possible to see a connection between the Priests and Levites and the modern day Pastors.

The idea that people bring in money to cover the costs of the running of the church building and to help the pastor spend more time in preparing the message etc., all makes sense and are good things to do. However, the pastor is no longer bound by the laws of the Priests and Levites.

Pastors are allowed to work for themselves. They are allowed to find other sources of income. It is very inconvenient and can often hinder their effectiveness, but there is nothing stopping them from doing it. As a pastor who wants to give my best to my congregation, as most pastors do, I have personally found, holding down a second job very difficult.

If a pastor chooses not to work to support their ministry, then they should be applauded for their faith in God's provision.

I believe that he (or she) should be honoured for their dedication to God's calling. However, the pressure they feel when they are short of cash because the congregation may not be giving enough to support them, should not be felt by the congregation.

The pastor needs to look to God for their provision, not to the congregation. It is not right when a pastor, feeling the stress of finances, puts pressure on people to meet their needs. Provision comes from God, and yes He regularly does use the congregation, but He doesn't have to.

Having said that, while the pastor should keep their sense of financial pressure off the congregation, I believe that the congregation should also honour the pastor in their giving.

> *"Let the elders who rule well be counted worthy of double honour, especially those who labour in the word and doctrine. For the Scripture says, 'You shall not muzzle an ox while it treads out the grain,' and 'The labourer is worthy of his wages.'" 1 Timothy 5:17-18*

It is hard for a pastor to have a second job when they want to give their best to their congregation. If the congregation wants the best from their pastor then they need to honour them with their finances.

Looking at the above passage in context we see that the reference of double honouring is in regards to wage or pay for work done.

This honouring should come as a result of the generous, honouring nature of Christ being manifest in the person. It shouldn't come from pressure or a sense of legal obligation.

I'll talk more about this in another chapter.

Another point here is that the church building is no longer the sacred place that the tithes and the offerings have to be taken to.

The primary purpose of the offering was for the cleansing of sin. The people had to bring an offering because there was no other way of getting rid of sin. The Priest sacrificed the offering and God gave permission to the priests to eat the offering.

The pastors do not spend all day offering continual sacrifices on behalf of the people.

> *"But this Man, after he had offered one sacrifice for sins forever, sat down at the right hand of God..."* Hebrews 10:12

Jesus sat down because the sacrificial work was complete, it was finished. There are no more sacrifices for sin.

> *"For there is one God and one Mediator between God and men, the Man, Christ Jesus."* 1 Timothy 2:5.

Each person is now responsible for their own right standing (righteousness) before God, and that can only be achieved by receiving the finished work of Jesus Christ at the cross.

> *'For He made Him who knew no sin to be sin for us, that we might become the righteousness (right standing) of God in Him.'* 2 Corinthians 5:21

The time of offerings for sin is finished and this is the kind of offering Malachi 3 speaks of. Salvation, righteousness, healing and blessing cannot be purchased from God. They are freely given by Him to those who accept the work of His Son.

Shepherd, feed the flock

The tithe mentioned in Malachi does provide for the Priests and Levites, but "all the tithe" also provides for the widow, the orphan and the stranger in the land. It also provides a feast for the entire household of the one bringing the tithe.

The ones who provided the tithe were land owners. They could afford to give their tithe (all 20%) and the offerings without them or their household going without. Others who were not wealthy, only had to focus on bringing to the temple that which would cleanse their sin.

Today's tithe is sometimes presented as a requirement for everybody to give, regardless of how much money they make, or what they may go without. The amount required is only 10% so it is not "all the tithe," and according to Malachi 3, it will not put people in a place to receive the blessing of God.

Notice also that the tithe required is the Levitical Tithe given to provide for the "Priests and the Levites" (aka, the church leader) and the upkeep of the temple (aka, the church building). There is no Feast Tithe or Poor Tithe.

> *"Thus says the Lord God to the shepherds: 'Woe to the shepherds of Israel who feed themselves! Should not the shepherd feed the flocks?'" Ezekiel 34:2b*

My belief is that if a pastor is requiring a tithe of people who are not in a financial position to give, in order to maintain their own wage or the church building, they are feeding themselves and not their sheep.

Please also understand here that there is a difference between being in a difficult financial position because of a lack of income and being in a difficult position because of a lack of budgeting skills or poor impulse control.

Some people who say they don't have money, do actually have money and they simply prioritise it in way that doesn't allow them to give to honour the pastor and support the church functions. Sometimes they just don't budget to allow the giving. These are not the situations I am talking about when I say 'financial difficulty.'

If a church preaches tithing, then it should divide the income up by the percentages as outlined by the Law.

50% of the income should go to running the church. That includes power, mortgage or rent, water, rates and wages. It should also include all the ministry areas, especially the worship team.

33% of the income should go back into the congregation celebrating and feasting. The congregation should not have to pay anything extra for that.

The last 17% should be channelled exclusively into charitable activities. Any overheads to pay for those activities such as wages, rent or equipment should come from the 50% part of the income.

The church should also remember that there are no tithes given at all every seventh year and so that should be budgeted for.

Sometimes the tithe message is presented in a way that says we are not under Law anymore, so we should adhere to the principles behind the Law. This means that when we look at Malachi 3, we don't have to be specific about how the tithes and offerings have to be given, just adhere to the principle that they should be given.

The message is that we do have a choice about whether or not we will give our tithes and offerings, because we don't live under Law ... but if we want to be blessed, we need to tithe. That is the choice implied by the message.

The message may not state it but there is another principle of Malachi 3: that if we don't tithe we will be cursed and if we don't tithe and give offerings we're robbing God. It can go a little further and may imply that it is really only the offering that gets us right with God and puts us in a position where we can ask things of Him.

As part of my research I listened to messages on tithing. I listened to one tithing message by a pastor of a very large church (I won't name him). In it he said that he would like to get rid of all the non-tithers from his church.

He said the reason why was because the non-tithers stopped the anointing of God flowing in the meeting. He said that not tithing blocks healing. He said that not tithing stops blessing. He then went on to say that tithing can secure a person's place in heaven.

There's not a lot of room for joy in that. In fact, this thinking makes giving a serious business. It puts a lot of pressure on us to give properly to please God and avoid being cursed. It can make us believe that tithing is the only way we have a right to expect good things from God.

> 'He shall see the labour of His soul and be satisfied. By His knowledge My righteous Servant shall justify many...' Isaiah 53:11

Did you read that? It is Jesus' labour that satisfies the Father, not ours. It is all about His hard work, His toil, His giving. It's not about us. That takes the pressure off us.

How about this? My intelligence, my knowledge of the Bible, how well I can work out 10% or even 22% isn't going to make me right before God. It is Jesus' knowledge. He bore my sins. He's the one who justifies me. He did it all. He covered everything.

That's exciting. I'm feeling more than a little bit cheerful. The giving I do or don't do has no impact on my relationship with God. I want to give. I don't have to give, but I want to. And when I do, I'm not going to resent it. I'm going to enjoy it.

Malachi 3 has absolutely no application to a church that lives under the New Covenant which was created through the shed blood of Jesus Christ. Its application and the principles found in Malachi are only for those who lived under the Law.

The problem with going back to those principles is that we misuse them because we take them out of context and we make ourselves legally liable if we fail in that part of the Law and that makes us guilty of breaking all the Law.

Because we live under the New Covenant, the Old Covenant (the Law) no longer applies to us. The principles of giving that we find under the New Covenant are very different in purpose and structure to the required giving of tithes and offerings that we find under the Law.

Chapter 5: How Jesus Gave

Jesus Didn't Tithe?

Even though the Bible's New Testament starts at Matthew, the New Covenant didn't actually begin until after the death of Jesus. Jesus was born under the Law. That was why He was born of Jewish descent. The Gentiles were not under the Law.

The Mosaic and Levitical Law was only given to the Jewish nation, not to any other nation. If a Gentile became a Proselyte to the Jewish religion, then that person became subject to the Law. So Jesus was born under the Law, He fulfilled the Law, He kept the Law. Jesus never sinned and He more than likely never paid tithes.

What? Jesus didn't tithe? But He kept the Law. That is exactly why He wouldn't have tithed, unless He grew his own crops. It was the Law. If He grew His own crops or herbs then He would have paid tithes on them.

So Jesus lived under the Law, He didn't pay tithes and He never sinned. We live under grace and if we don't tithe, we're often left feeling like we have sinned. It usually isn't the gentle prompting of the Holy Spirit either.

My experience and the experiences others have related to me have been of fear, guilt and condemnation. These aren't feelings that come from God and they don't come from being in grace. Every pastor I know would be devastated if they thought they caused it, so it's not them.

These are feelings associated with the enemy when we sin. Some people may say that those feelings make sense because not paying tithes is a sin. But where does the Bible say that not paying tithes is a sin?

Is it Malachi where it says that not paying tithes is robbing God? We've already seen that we're not robbing God by not paying tithes.

Is it the Law? We don't live under the Law.

Is it because Abram and Jacob paid tithes, sort of?

We've looked at those and they certainly didn't set a precedence for the modern day version of tithes. In fact they didn't set any precedent.

Does Paul list 'not tithing' as a work of the flesh? Does he include it in with other behaviours that will stop us from entering the kingdom? Do any other authors of the New Testament list it? I don't believe they do.

Is it because it was so obvious the Bible authors didn't need to say it? The authors had ample opportunity to introduce tithing into cultures that didn't tithe, where it was not common or obvious, and they didn't say anything.

Did Jesus set a law for us to tithe? We will look at what Jesus thinks about giving and see that He doesn't.

So how did 'not tithing' become sinning? It's certainly not Biblical.

The truth is that it is not a sin not to tithe. It's not. We don't need forgiveness if we don't tithe. We're not robbing God if we don't tithe. We don't have to make it up the next week if we miss paying. We won't come under a curse if we don't pay our tithe. We don't have to pay tithes in advance if we're going to be away on holiday, so we don't miss them. ***It's not a sin to not***

pay tithes. Relax. Take a deep breath and move into some freedom.

It's increase, not income

Luke 11:42 and Matthew 23:23 relate an instance when Jesus rebuked the scribes and Pharisees. The nature of the rebuke was that the scribes and Pharisees spent so much effort making sure they met the exact behaviours of the Law that they neglected the spirit of it; justice, mercy and faith.

Both of these passages use the tithe of small herbs as the example of meeting the exact requirements of the Law. Jesus does not finish there though. He is very specific when He says, 'These (justice, mercy and faith) you ought to have done, without leaving the others (tithing the herbs) undone.'

But doesn't that support the argument for tithing? Absolutely; *if we lived under the Law*. We need to remember the Pharisees were very good at living under the law. In fact, paying herbs as tithes was not originally required by the Law.

John Gill states that it was a common saying or maxim among Jews that 'the tithing of corn is from the law, but the tithing of herbs is from the Rabbins.' The

Tractate Ma'aseroth, Chapter 1, Mishna 1 expands the tithing of the 'fruits of the earth' to include having to pay a tithe on any plant that could be used as a food and was grown in a contained area.

This enabled the Pharisees to pay tithes on produce if they weren't land holders. They could pay tithes on their kitchen herbs. This was another area they could keep the Law in and appear more righteous.

Remember also that tithing was given on the increase, not the income. The Pharisees who tithed on the mint and cumin would also have had jobs, like Paul and tent making. They did not tithe on what they earned from their jobs. They tithed on what they grew and what they grew was not used for income. It was used for tithing … and possibly flavouring food.

Justice, mercy and faith

The point that Jesus was making in these passages is not that everyone should be tithing. It was that the Pharisees focused so much on meeting the fine print of the Law in terms of behaviour that they forgot the heart of the Law.

The purpose of the Law was to provide justice, mercy and faith. The Pharisees, in meeting the behavioural requirement of the Law, neglected the attitudes the Law was created for.

Today's version of the tithe is **10% of our income (not increase), given on a regular and ongoing basis, from whatever the source of income, no matter what socio-economic group the person is in**. The modern tithe is usually associated with the 10% used for the running of the temple/tabernacle and the feeding or payment of the Priests and Levites.

There are two tithes not spoken about. These tithes are the ones that celebrate God's blessing and provide for the widows, the orphans and the strangers in the land. The two tithes that aren't included are the two tithes that are closest to God's heart. They are the ones that truly show justice, mercy and faith.

Have we become like the Pharisees? Do we emphasise the things that allow us to be showy? Do we neglect the weightier matters such as justice, mercy and faith?

The righteous value of tithing

In Luke 18:9-12, Jesus expands His view on Pharisees and the value He placed on their tithes. This is the parable where Jesus compares a Pharisee and a tax collector. The Pharisee stands secure in his righteousness based on his fasting and tithing. The tax collector throws himself on the mercy of God. According to Jesus, it is the tax collector who goes away justified, not the Pharisee.

A Pharisee would base their righteousness on their ability to keep all the physical requirements of the Law. Those whose salvation rests on the finished work of Jesus at the cross are made righteous by faith.

> *"For He (God the Father) made Him who knew no sin (God the Son, Jesus Christ) to be sin for us, that we might become the righteousness of God in Him (Jesus)." 2 Corinthians 5:21*

This is how our righteousness exceeds the righteousness of the scribes and Pharisees. Our righteousness is the righteousness of God not the righteousness of our own works.

Our righteousness is not dependent on our giving. Being blessed does not depend on our efforts. Remember, it is *all* about Jesus. Can you feel weight lift off your shoulders?

Render to Caesar...

The three synoptic gospels all have a story of men trying to trick Jesus in regards to taxes. They asked Him if it was lawful for Jews to pay taxes. Jesus had them pull out a coin and tell them whose face was on it. They replied that Caesar's face was. Jesus then said, 'Render therefore to Caesar the things that are Caesar's, and to God the things that are God's.'

Some have said that Jesus is saying to pay our taxes first and then pay the 10% from what is left. Perhaps there is an underlying implication in the question posed to Jesus. Perhaps the men were really asking if they should pay the full amount of tithes plus the poll tax.

In truth, the ones who asked the question didn't care about that. A number of the questioners would not have had to tithe anyway since it was only required of those who grew crops and raised flocks. They were asking a question designed to trap Jesus and label Him as someone leading an uprising against the Roman Empire. It was not about tithing.

I suppose there might be a case here for not giving *any* money to God. After all, Jesus said to give the money to the one whose face was printed on it. Jesus told Pilate that His kingdom was not of this world, and as far as I'm aware, the currency of the kingdom of God is not printed on metal (or paper or plastic).

Perhaps Jesus was simply saying that our lives belong to God and we should give Him honour by doing the right thing with the laws of the land we live under.

The widow's two mites

Luke 21:1-4 is a passage used often to show Jesus' attitude toward giving. It is the passage of the widow's two mites. In the passage we see a widow, who in Jesus' view, gives more than anyone else, because she had nothing to give out of. She deposits two mites into the temple treasury.

We don't know if this was a voluntary payment or the mandatory payment made yearly for the service of the temple and to support the poor. What we do know is that she gave all that she had and those two mites were more valuable to God than the rich gifts the others were depositing.

I have heard this passage, or its parallel in Mark 12:41-44 referred to when a giving message is preached. I've even used it myself. The reference is usually about giving even when we have nothing and that God will honour it.

I believed I should give in faith even when I didn't think I had enough. I believed God would repay me for the sacrifice I made. I now have confidence that God will repay us for the sacrifices we make, when He is the One who asked us to make them.

The widow's sacrificial giving is highlighted and honoured. A problem here though is that the only honour Jesus gives the woman is to say that she gave more than the others. We don't see any promise of a return for her sacrifice. We don't hear of a promise of greater honour coming in heaven.

It is interesting and important to note the context of this part in the life of Christ. We read in Luke 20:46-47 and in Mark 12:38-40 how Jesus warned the disciples about the scribes. The scribes were interpreters, teachers and enforcers of the law who held authority in the Jewish culture.

Jesus warns that the scribes love to appear holy and religious but it is a façade. The love of God is not in them. Jesus makes a point of saying that they 'devour widow's houses.' Their interpretations of the law and their enforcing of it caused those who were supposed to be looked after by the law, to lose all that they had.

As if to emphasise their corruption of the law, Jesus points out a poor woman who has to give the last bit of money she has to support the temple building program. We know the money was going to the program because as Jesus and His disciples are leaving the temple, one of His disciples makes a comment about it (Mark 13:1).

The disciple points out how beautiful the temple is, because of the building program. Jesus responds by saying that the temple will be torn apart in the not too distant future.

In context, we see that the story of the woman with two mites is *more* than honouring those who give out of lack. It seems that it is also a denunciation of those who coerce people who lack, to give all they have to pay for something that won't last.

I wonder how many times the story of the woman with two mites has been used to convince people without much to give to a building program leaving them with difficulty paying their own rent.

Would Jesus then say to those who comment about how beautiful the church building looks, that it won't be long before one stone no longer remains on the other and that the money would have been better spent on those who needed it instead of taking it from them.

The sons are free

On only one occasion that I am aware of, is Jesus seen playing a part in the giving of money. We see Him give food (loaves and fish), He gives life, He gives blessing, He gives healing, wisdom and the Holy Spirit. We also see Him give His own life but the occasions where Jesus gives money are very rare.

We know He received money and gifts because the disciples had a money box kept by Judas Iscariot. It is possible they gave to the poor, although there is nothing in the Bible that out rightly says they did.

Jesus encouraged giving to others and not expecting a return so we could assume that He did that Himself. It would seem that not much money was given however, because Judas would take the money that was put in the money box.

The occasion where Jesus participated in the payment of money is found in Matthew 17:24-27. Peter is asked if Jesus pays the required 'voluntary' Temple Tax. Peter says yes, but doesn't really know.

The Temple Tax was used to pay for various articles to help keep the temple running. To follow the train of thought of those preaching tithing, we can spiritualise this as it took place before the crucifixion of Jesus. That means we can substitute the word church in place of temple.

This means, that the congregation was required to 'voluntarily' pay a certain amount of money to keep the church running. In Jesus day it was called the Temple Tax. Some would think that it might coincide with tithes and offerings but since it was only required once a year it would probably be called a miracle offering.

So Peter returns to the house in which they were staying, wondering if Jesus contributes to the miracle offering each year.

Jesus, knowing what had happened, asked Peter (Simon) 'From whom do the kings of the earth take customs or taxes, from their sons or from strangers?'

Peter replies, 'From strangers.'

Jesus says to Peter, 'Then the sons are free.'

Jesus implies that the pressure for finances to maintain the running of the church should not be placed on the members of the congregation. The kings of the earth don't put financial pressure on their own families and it seems that the King of Heaven doesn't either. His children are free.

After Jesus tells Peter that the sons are free, He then instructs Peter to catch a fish, open its mouth and use the money inside for the temple tax. Jesus does this, not because of an obligation to pay, but in order to avoid causing offence.

This is a true miracle offering. Often, but not always, a miracle offering means the members of the congregation will give and are told a miracle of provision will come after giving. When Jesus does miracle offerings, He receives the miracle of provision first and gives from that.

Miracle provision

I was very excited to hear of a miracle offering set up in one church. It worked like this. The pastor announced at the start of the year that a miracle offering was coming at the end of the year. The congregation were encouraged to ask God for the figure He wanted them to give. After they received the figure, they then believed that God would provide it before the end of the year.

The congregation were asked not to put it aside from weekly earnings, but were to look for unusual supplies of finances beyond their regular source. They were to look for the miracle provision. The testimonies were amazing.

Having said that, there is nothing wrong with putting aside money for an upcoming offering. It just wasn't how the pastor felt God wanted it done that time, perhaps to exercise the faith of the congregation.

Paul encourages the church at Corinth to put money aside. 1 Corinthians 16:2 has Paul telling the church to put money aside the first day of the week so it is ready for the offering going to the church in Jerusalem. I will talk about this more in the next chapter.

The first miracle of provision we see in the life of Jesus is not long after His birth. Wise men came to Jesus bearing gifts of gold, frankincense and myrrh. It is interesting to note that the wise men were astrologers, pagan priests. God will use whomever He chooses to bring the provision we need. Some of those sources may be quite unexpected.

Another example of miracle provision is seen where Jesus feeds the five thousand and then the four thousand. I have preached messages on the generosity of the lad who presented the loaves and fish to Jesus.

In the account of the feeding of the four thousand it was the disciples who gave the loaves and fish (they are two separate incidents as Matthew has an account of both of them). I have to wonder though if my focus was on the wrong people in the stories.

Perhaps the lad and the disciples were incidental to the story. Perhaps they were merely the vessels God used to get the miracle provision into the hands of Jesus. What if, when we read the gospels, our focus stays fixed on Jesus?

Gavin Tooley opened my eyes to this concept in a message he gave at our church one time. He said that the disciples and other people mentioned in the gospels are examples of pre-Christians. They show us who we were before salvation. They do not show us the new creation. We need to look at Jesus for that and use Him as our example.

As new creations, the Holy Spirit is transforming us from glory to glory, into the image of the Son, not the image of the disciples.

In both stories of feeding the multitudes, we see Jesus receiving miracle provision and then multiplying it to provide for thousands of people. After everyone had eaten there was also an abundance left over. Since Jesus is our example, the One whose image we are being conformed to, perhaps our giving should be more like His.

What kind of giving was Jesus into?

When Jesus taught about giving, amounts and percentages never came into it. He always taught that giving, as with any behaviour, comes from the heart. When Jesus gave, He gave His all from a heart of generosity. He held nothing back. He gave out of intimacy with the Father, having an absolute assurance that the Father was His provider.

In Matthew chapter 5 Jesus addresses heart issues. He preaches that the attitude of the heart is as real to the Father as the actual behaviour.

If a man looks at a woman with lust, he's already committed adultery. If you're angry with your brother without cause, you've already committed murder. Don't go bringing an offering to the temple if your brother has something against you. Deal with the heart issue first and then present your offering.

> *"But love your enemies, do good and lend,*
> *hoping for nothing in return; and your*
> *reward will be great, and you will be sons of*
> *the Most High. For He is kind to the*
> *unthankful and evil." Luke 6:35*

This giving stems from a heart attitude. It is the attitude of the Father.

The word translated here as 'sons,' literally means, 'like.'

Jesus is not saying that you have to carry out those particular behaviours in order to earn your place as a son of God. He is saying that if you do those things then you will show yourself to be 'like' the Father, who causes it to rain (that is, He blesses, or opens the windows of heaven) on the just and the unjust alike. He is kind to the unthankful and evil.

Jesus tells us that we are to love, do good and lend to others, not because of what we will get back, but because it is the character or nature of God. As new creations we are partakers of His divine nature and we will naturally act like he does, because we are like Him. It is all about the heart.

We are to give like Jesus gave. He received miracle provision, multiplied what He'd received and gave abundantly from that. Jesus never questioned whether or not He could afford to do something because He assumed that if the Father wanted Him to do it, the Father would provide.

One reason we may not experience miracle provision is because sometimes we are not doing God things. It is possible to do a good thing, but that's not the same as a God thing.

Jesus said:

> *"Most assuredly, I say to you, the Son can do nothing of Himself, but what He sees the Father do; for whatever He does, the Son also does in like manner." John 5:19*

Jesus limited His activities to doing the things He saw the Father do. There are many good causes we could be involved in, but we should limit ourselves to the ones we know that Father has planned for us. He probably has someone else in mind to do something He hasn't asked us to do. God will provide when His will and ours are knit together.

God is 'The Lord Will Provide.' If we are doing something that He's asked us to do, He will provide.

That provision may not look like what we want it to or how we expect it to, but it will come.

What we need is faith.

> *"So then faith comes by hearing and hearing by the word of God." Romans 10:17*

This passage is primarily talking about the spreading of the gospel, but I believe it can be used this way as well.

Faith literally means, 'God's divine persuasion.' Faith is not something we summon or convince ourselves of. It is not forcing ourselves to accept something and it is not quoting scripture over and over again.

Faith has nothing to do with us. Faith is an act of God. He persuades us of a truth through revelation. When Jesus was walking on this earth, He lived in faith. He was divinely persuaded that God the Father is 'The Lord Will Provide.'

When Jesus was being tempted by Satan in the wilderness, the devil tried to have Jesus doubt the Father's provision.

"Hey Jesus. You're hungry. If You're really God's Son, how come He's let You go hungry? He's holding out on You. Turn these stones into bread. Feed yourself."

"Hey Devil. If He's not giving me food yet, it's because it's not a need. If I needed it, He'd give it to me. Man doesn't live on bread alone anyway, but on the rhema (revelation) word of God."

Did you get that? If your provision hasn't come yet, it could be because you don't need it yet. God supplies all of our needs. We're His children, His sons. That means if a need isn't being met, it's not really a need. We just think it is. Or we're being made to believe it is so the devil can convince us God's holding out on us. There's a bit of freedom there.

Chapter 6: How The Early Church Gave

Heart Transformation

The heart transformation we see in the early church is amazing. Jesus had been crucified, buried, resurrected and ascended to heaven and the Holy Spirit had come with power on the Day of Pentecost. The Law had been fulfilled in its entirety. Jesus was recognised by the believers (called 'Followers of the Way' at the time) as the Messiah.

Since the first believers were for the most part, Jewish, they continued to follow the Law, not understanding yet the full freedom that Jesus had brought them into. They encountered love for each other and for God as never experienced before.

Relationship with God as Father became real, their hearts of stone had been replaced with hearts of flesh and they knew that Jesus had ripped open the temple veil, allowing them access into the Holy of Holies. Generosity overwhelmed them.

Generosity

Acts 2:44-45 tells us that all those who believed were together and had all things in common and sold their possessions and goods and divided them among all, as anyone had need.

These were spontaneous acts of generosity, inspired by the Holy Spirit and the love of God. No-one lacked because anyone who did was simply given what they needed. There was no obligation, no requirement, no saying that it's important to give and 10% is a great place to start. Generosity simply burst out them as a reflection of the heart of the Father.

The end of Acts 4 expands on this. People sold land and houses and brought the proceeds to the apostles for them to distribute. People lost their possessiveness and sense of entitlement.

They gave 100%, not 10%. They didn't consider anything they had as their own, but simply as tools that could be used to show the love of God to others. The proof that there was no obligation in this is seen in Acts 5 in the account of Ananias and Sapphira.

Ananias and Sapphira sold some land and kept back part of the proceeds but laid the rest at the apostle's feet. The issue is that they lied about how much they sold it for. Peter asks Ananias why he lied to the Holy Spirit and kept back part of the price of the land for themselves.

Peter asked Ananias a question about his land.

> *"While it remained, was it not your own? And after it was sold, was it not in your control?" Acts 5:4*

Peter is saying there was no obligation to sell the land and no obligation to bring the proceeds in if they didn't want to. The issue was in the fact that they sold the land for a certain price and lied saying that they were bringing in the whole amount from the sale.

Whatever the reason for Ananias and Sapphira lying, they paid a high price for it. Remember, it was because they lied, not because they didn't bring the whole amount of the land sale.

People were so excited about Jesus that news spread out of the Jewish people groups to the Gentiles. Here was a problem for the Jews. Their Law meant that contact with Gentiles made them unclean.

The Jerusalem Council

Peter received a vision that challenged this concept and was told quite firmly that what God had cleansed, should not be called common or unclean. Even though the believing Jews still followed the Law, their understanding of it was being changed. The gospel spread to the Gentiles and another problem arose. What laws should be given to the believing Gentiles?

Acts 15 recounts that certain believing Pharisees had said it was necessary that the Gentile converts be circumcised and keep the Law of Moses in order to be saved.

At the Jerusalem Council Peter asked why they were testing God:

> *"...by putting a yoke on the neck of the disciples that neither our fathers nor we were able to bear? But we believe that through the grace of the Lord Jesus Christ we shall be saved in the same manner as they." Acts 15:10-11*

I believe that it was this declaration that brought the revelation that salvation came from grace alone, separate from the law. Peter says that the Gentiles will not be saved by being like the Jews. The Jews will be saved by being like the Gentiles; saved by grace and not by meeting the requirements of the Law.

The decision the apostles, elders and brethren came to was this:

> *"For it seemed good to the Holy Spirit, and to us, to lay upon you no greater burden than these necessary things: that you abstain from things offered to idols, from blood, from things strangled and from sexual immorality." Acts 15:28-29*

There was a great opportunity to continue the tithing regulations here. Already Gentiles were looking at being circumcised and embracing the Law. It would not have been difficult to cement the giving of tithes. But they didn't.

It seemed good to the Holy Spirit Himself and the first apostles not to mention anything about tithing. They didn't mention anything about the Sabbath. They didn't mention anything about Feasts or bacon. They didn't mention anything about ritual cleansing. They didn't even say not to worry about circumcision.

They (including the Holy Spirit) said that out of all the Law of Moses the Gentiles could do, they should only concern themselves with staying away from the four things previously mentioned. These, they said were necessary. Everything else not mentioned was obviously not considered necessary.

Wait a second. Tithing wasn't in the list of necessary things? Tithing was unnecessary? It seemed good to the **Holy Spirit** for the Gentiles not to tithe. It seemed *good* to the Holy Spirit for the Gentiles not to tithe. It seemed *good* to the **Holy Spirit** for the Gentiles *not* to *tithe.* If God thought it was good for us as Gentiles not to tithe, then who thought it was good for us *to* tithe?

The first Apostles, the men who spent years with Jesus, physically interacting with Him night and day, felt that it was good for us not to tithe. In fact they said that tithes and the rest of the Law was a yoke that was too great for them and their fathers to bear. *They* said not to give the Gentiles the Law.

So who gave us the Law in the New Covenant? Who gave us tithing in the present times? It wasn't God and it wasn't the first Apostles. It wasn't Paul.

(**Please note:** I have known many good pastors who preached tithing with a sincere heart. I used to preach

118

tithing before becoming a pastor. The men and women I knew who preached tithing, did it believing wholeheartedly that tithing was of great benefit to the tither. They also believed that it was the will of God for them and others.)

Who wants to put a yoke on us that is too great to bear? Who wants to steal away our freedom and bring us into ritualism and condemnation? Who wants to destroy our trust in God as a loving Father and as 'The Lord Will Provide?'

The following paragraphs are the answers that leapt out at me when I asked myself the above questions. They are *not* a reflection of people who preach tithing.

Most people who believe in tithing and preach it are doing so because they want the best for the people they are speaking to. I don't want to belittle them or bring condemnation to them and I don't want to promote myself above them because I am not.

What I am hoping to do is to expose a deception of the enemy. If the enemy can find a way to rob the church of its liberty, he will. If the enemy can find a way to take us out of the freedom of the gospel and into the bondage of religion, he will. If the enemy can find a way to tie us up in ritualism, condemnation and lack of relationship with the Father, he will. If my answers *are* right then I believe the truth needs to be revealed.

Remember that our enemy is a counterfeiter. He copies everything God meant for good and twists it into something that may look right but ultimately brings bondage and condemnation. Originally, the tithe was meant to help people.

The tithe was a tax and social welfare system. It provided for those less able to provide for themselves. It did it in a way that didn't disadvantage or put pressure on the giver.

Remember also, there is no tithe in the Bible comparable with the tithe we work with today. Before God gave the Law to Moses, outside the Bible, tithing was a governmental tax or levy system.

In the Bible, with Abram (Abraham) it was a once-only event, using someone else's money.

The tithe with Jacob was a promise we never see acted on and conditional upon God fulfilling the wants of Jacob. It was also associated with a reduction of the blessing promised by God.

After the introduction of the Law, the tithe was 20% of a farmers increase (or 22% if paying cash) on either crops or livestock. It was only given after harvest and only for six out of seven years. It wasn't required of everybody, only those with crops or livestock. It was especially not required of people in financial difficulty. The tithe was to help those people.

Today's tithe is **the ongoing, regular giving of ten percent of a person's income,** regardless of how it came to them and regardless of the financial position they're in.

Today's tithe is a counterfeit of the original. It has been twisted into something that can bring bondage and condemnation.

Without faith it's impossible to please God

Romans chapter 14 is all about food and faith. Paul basically says that whether or not you eat certain foods (such as meat that may have been offered to idols) is not important.

What your faith allows you to do is important, but even more important than that is to not allow the faith and liberty you have to be a stumbling block or an offence to someone else. It is certainly important not to look down on a person who doesn't have the faith you have.

This was a message to both Jewish and Gentile Christians. Paul's message to the Roman Christians was effectively throwing away concern over three of the four things to abstain from as given by the Council of Jerusalem. Paul never wavered on the last issue I believe, because of the emotional, physical and spiritual consequences of sexual immorality.

Tithing in Hebrews

The only time tithing is mentioned outside of the gospels in the New Testament is in the book of Hebrews. The references occur in chapter seven.

The book of Hebrews was written before the temple was destroyed. There were still tithes being brought in, sacrifices being made and offerings given. The book was directed primarily to Jewish Christians, probably in Jerusalem.

The focus of the message of Hebrews is really to help the Jewish Christians move in faith to a place of deeper revelation of the New Covenant they have in Christ. It is the covenant that was promised in the Old Testament scriptures.

The Jewish Christians at the time were still living under the Law. They continued to make sacrifices and give tithes. The author clearly points out that there is no more need for sacrifices, as the law had been completely fulfilled and that the High Priest is now seated, having perfected forever, those who are being sanctified (Hebrews 10).

Hebrews 7:5 says that the sons of Levi had a commandment to receive tithes from the people 'according to the law.' Again, the reference to tithing as an ongoing tradition in Hebrews is under the Law.

There is a reference in verse 8 to men receiving tithes here, and there, he (Melchizedek) receives them. This 'there' is actually referring to the time that Melchizedek received tithes from Abraham, not 'there' as in Jesus receiving them in heaven.

The author then points out that the Law they lived under was unable to bring perfection because the priesthood was imperfect. There was, out of necessity a change of priesthood away from the Levites to the order of Melchizedek.

> *"For the priesthood being changed, of necessity there is also a change of the law."*
> Hebrews 7:12

The Law of Moses is referred to as having been annulled (Hebrews 7:18) and made obsolete (Hebrews

8:13). Because the priesthood changed, the law changed.

This meant that the Law of Moses is annulled, which literally means a cancellation or no longer in effect. That means that tithing according to the Law has been cancelled and no longer in effect.

So what about the new law? Does the new law of Melchizedek have any tithing in it? Abraham did pay tithes to Melchizedek, as a one off incident, with other people's money. Do we set precedence with that? Since Melchizedek is really described in Hebrews as foreshadowing Christ, perhaps, rather than looking at Abraham, we should look at Jesus Christ and His law.

Christ's commands

As far as I am aware, nowhere does Jesus stipulate that we, as believers, under His new covenant need to pay tithes. Galatians 6:2 tells us that bearing one another's burdens fulfils the law of Christ. The seven basic commandments of Jesus are to love one another, pray for our enemies, repent, believe that Jesus is in the Father, take up our cross and follow Him, go and make disciples and pray always (not pay always).

Pay the pastor?

Should the pastor be paid for being a pastor?

In 1 Corinthians 9, Paul speaks about being paid if you work full time, preaching the gospel.

> *"If we have sown spiritual things for you, is it a great thing if we reap your material things?" 1 Corinthians 9:11*

> *"Even so the Lord has commanded that those who preach the gospel should live from the gospel." 1 Corinthians 9:14*

Here is the perfect opportunity for Paul to say that the amount that each person should give is 10%. But he doesn't say anything.

Paul says something similar in Galatians.

> *"Let him who is taught the word share in all good things with him who teaches." Galatians 6:6*

Again, Paul could say that a good starting place would be 10% of your income. But he doesn't. He doesn't say anything about a tithe.

Paul implies that if a pastor is paid by the church, the money comes from purely voluntary giving out of the generosity and thankfulness of those who have received spiritual things.

Paul encourages the congregation to pay their pastors. As the passage in 1 Timothy 5:17-18 says, they are worthy even of double honour (wages). This book is not about refusing to pay our pastors, it's about giving in faith and with a cheerful heart. It's about receiving revelation of God the Father as 'The Lord Will Provide.'

The comments in the book are primarily about moving away from giving out of ritualism to a place of giving out of our relationship with our Father. They are to break us free from the unbiblical modern concept of tithing.

1 Corinthians 9:15 has Paul saying that he used none of those rights. Paul continued working as a tent maker, earning his own income. In verse 18 Paul declares that the reward he has for not using his rights to an income was that he could present the gospel of Christ without charge and not abuse his authority in the gospel.

Spiritual abuse

There is an implication that those who rely on being paid by the church *can* slip into an abusive way of convincing the congregation to give. There have been times when we have not received much money from our offerings in church. I knew we needed money for rent and other bills and I thought of things I could say in a giving message that would convince the congregation to give more.

However, I realised that the messages came from me and not God. They would have been manipulative in nature. This is abuse and on those days I chose not to give a message. I decided I would rather trust God to supply than to bring the ones God had entrusted me with into the Law and abusive bondage.

Offerings

The Apostle Paul spent a fair bit of his time raising funds for the church in Jerusalem. The area was in famine and Paul was encouraging other churches to help the Christians there with financial gifts.

Some of the passages from 1 and 2 Corinthians involving the giving of money were references to the offering promised by the church at Corinth for the church in Jerusalem. Other passages were to do with supporting the pastor in a local church. The one below is about the offering for Jerusalem.

> *"On the first day of the week let each one of you lay something aside, storing up as he may prosper, that there be no collections when I come." 1 Corinthians 16:2*

This passage has been used to promote the idea of Sunday collections.

As I have said, there is nothing wrong with Sunday collections. There is nothing wrong with financially supporting the pastor of your local church. In fact Paul says it is a good thing to do, and the right thing to do. He is speaking to those who are receiving spiritual things from the pastor. He is encouraging voluntary giving. He is not speaking to the pastor for them to put pressure on the congregation.

The above passage however, is not related to supporting the pastor. Paul is simply encouraging the church at Corinth to be ready for him when he comes to collect the offering for Jerusalem.

The Corinthian church had promised a certain amount and Paul wanted to make sure they were going to have it. He didn't want to have to put pressure on anyone when he arrived by having lots of offerings then. He didn't want anyone to go without in order to meet their promised commitment.

Paul's suggestion of putting aside some money on the first day of the week was a practical way of making sure everyone could give as much as they promised. Notice also that the offering was to be given out of prosperity, 'storing up as he may prosper.'

In essence, this is like the miracle offering I mentioned earlier. It was not waiting for the big cheque, but putting aside the little bits as God gave miracle provision.

This is not a passage that says everyone should pay money each Sunday in order to keep the church running and pay the pastor. Are there principles that can be used here about regular giving in church? Yes, but not to the detriment of the giver. And not to bring the giver into a place of ritualism and bondage.

Paul encouraged freedom in giving. In 2 Corinthians Paul continues to address the church in regards to the offering. Some people had sown doubt in the minds of the Corinthian Christians as to the motives of Paul collecting the money. They began to think Paul was going to use it for something other than what he had said he would.

In 2 Corinthians 9 Paul speaks to the church giving them principles of giving. Again, he asks them to prepare the offering beforehand so the giving doesn't become a burden when he collects it.

I have been in conferences that have gone on for many days and every day an offering was received. At first I was generous because I love giving, but after a while, it became a burden and when I gave, I gave grudgingly.

This is what Paul was trying to avoid by asking them to put aside a little each week. He wants them to maintain their attitude of generosity and not let their giving come from an attitude of grudging obligation. Because God loves a cheerful giver. God is interested in the heart attitude far more than He is in behaviours.

> *"So let each one give as he purposes in his heart, not grudgingly or of necessity; for God loves a cheerful giver." 2 Corinthians 9:7*

Giving in the New Testament did not involve giving a set amount or a percentage. It involved giving freely from a heart of generosity that came as a result of the transforming work of the Holy Spirit. The amount to be given, for whatever purpose, was determined by the desire of the individual in consultation with the Holy Spirit.

They did not give unwillingly or from a place of feeling forced into it. They did not give as a result of obligation, rules or feeling like they had to, in order to receive something from God. They gave cheerfully from a place of prospering.

They gave willingly with a good attitude. I believe that the implication here is that God would rather we not give if we have a bad attitude that goes with it. God doesn't want that attitude to remain though because it isn't part of His character. God has a generous nature and He loves to give.

Chapter 7: Giving Under Grace

It's All God's

There is very clear evidence from the Bible that there is no requirement for Christians to tithe. There is however a lot of teaching in the New Testament about generous, abundant, even extravagant giving. There's teaching about giving freely without thought of reward. There's teaching about stewardship. There's teaching on faith. It's all about giving under grace.

Under grace, we're not limiting ourselves to a 10% tithe, plus an offering. Under grace, Jesus raises the bar. Under Law, if we were physically 'intimate' with someone who was not our spouse, we committed adultery. Under grace, if we lust after someone who is not our spouse we commit adultery.

Under Law we could get away with wrong attitudes and thoughts as long as our actions were lawful. Under grace, even our thoughts and attitudes are meant to be righteous. Under grace everything is 100%. It's 100% God. It's not 10% God and 90% us. Everything is about Him.

It's my understanding that under grace, 100% of everything we have and everything we are is surrendered to the purposes of God. All of it. Money, job, material goods, family and even our own lives. All of it is surrendered to Him. This of course leaves us with the responsibility of joining our will to His so we use what we've surrendered for His purposes.

I have based the following points on an assumption that you as the reader are managing your finances well. You have your priorities of spending sorted out and your heart is for God's purposes in relation to finances.

One of the great traps in western culture is to spend more than we make. We attempt to live a lifestyle that is beyond our means. When we get a pay rise, instead of putting the extra money aside to invest, we increase our spending. Now, there is nothing wrong with having nice things. The question is whether or not you spoke to God about it before you bought it?

Money is a tool

Money is not evil. Money is an object. It is neither good nor evil. It is a tool for both but of itself it is neither. The love of money is not the root of all evil.

> *"For the love of money is **a** root of all **kinds of** evil, for which some have strayed from the faith in their greediness and pierced themselves through with many sorrows."* 1 Timothy 6:10

The wrong attitudes towards money can cause much trouble in a person's life. Jesus said that we can't serve two masters making mention of both God and mammon. There is plenty of discussion of what mammon is. Some say it's money. Some say it's a spirit or an old god.

Regardless of what mammon actually is, the concept behind what Jesus said was that it is very hard for us to serve God if we are worried about where our provision will come from. We need to trust God as our provider.

God is our provider

If God asks us to give our house away, we do it and rely on Him to provide what we need. If we are more worried about money and don't trust God's ability to provide, we simply won't do it.

In a number of ways, tithing can undermine this trust. Tithing says that 10% of what we earn belongs to God. This leaves 90% that is ours to do what we want with. Anything we do with that 90% that contributes to the Kingdom of God is really a bonus for Him, and comes from our goodness.

I believe that we give 100% to God. When we surrender it to Him it's all His. One of the things we surrender to God is our will. When going for a job, do we look for the highest paying job or a job that is God's will for us? They might be the same, but they might not be.

I applied for a job as a school chaplain in 2010. I thought it would be a great job. The pay was good, the hours suited me and it was in a ministry role. I felt sure that God would want me to have that job but I didn't actually check with Him.

I didn't get the job and I complained bitterly to God for some time about it. I felt I was more qualified than the other people I knew who also applied for the job. I felt it was unfair.

A couple of months later, the opportunity came to begin pastoring at a church in Cessnock. At the time of writing this book I have been here for over five years. If I had been successful with the other job, I would never have taken this opportunity. I was looking for security not God's will.

I know that the pay is not as good (at the moment) as the school chaplaincy position would have been but I have never had such amazing job satisfaction as I do now. I have also never before experienced the miraculous provision I do now.

I didn't check with God about what He wanted me to do, but I guess because I had surrendered my life to Him, He made sure I stayed in His will. I didn't know it at the time and I was upset about it, but now I am so glad He did it.

We need to have a revelation that God is our provider. He may use a job, the church or even a random stranger to get money into our hands. Nothing is impossible for Him. It means that if we lose a job, for reasons other than being a bad employee, we can trust God to find another way to provide for us. If you are a pastor and the offerings are small, another way of provision will open up. Only believe.

Seek His kingdom first and God will provide. This does not mean to give 10% before the bills are paid. It means to seek God's will in regards to the money we have. It speaks of not allowing money to control what we do.

I have often asked God how much He wants me to give and He sometimes asks me to give more than I think I have. I have learnt that when He asks me to give (as opposed to people asking), He always provides.

Prosperity

There are many reasons why people don't appear to be prospering. One reason could be because of our understanding of prosperity. For some of us in the western world, prosperity means a four bedroom house, three cars, a TV in every room and a swimming pool in the back yard.

In a third world country, prosperity could be having a goat, even though the family lives in a drain. Prosperity is really about having enough to pay your bills (which are managed carefully), provide for our family, now and in the future and still be able to give to others. 2 Corinthians 9:8 tells us that God will provide so that we have enough in all things and also have an abundance for every good work.

Another reason for lack of apparent prosperity could be because we've made some bad choices or manage money poorly. Another reason could be the season we are in.

In Philippians 4:12, Paul says that he learned to be abased and he knew how to abound. There were times when Paul had nothing and times when he had an abundance. He knew how to be content no matter what his circumstances.

In verse 13, in relation to his state of need, or lack of need, he says that he could do all things through Christ who strengthened him. In Christ, he was content in any situation.

Paul was a man who lived in a full revelation of the grace and favour of God. He lived in God's blessing, but God's blessing doesn't always look like a four bedroom house with ducted air conditioning and a pool.

2 Corinthians 11:24-28 give us a list of some of the experiences that Paul went through during his life. He received thirty nine stripes on five separate occasions. He was beaten with rods on three occasions.

Paul was stoned once and mostly likely died but was raised from the dead to continue his work. He was shipwrecked three times. He was imprisoned a number of times. He was in constant peril from people and nature. He was regularly sleepless, hungry and thirsty. He was often cold and naked. Ultimately he was beheaded.

I've been upset in the past because I didn't get the job I wanted or I had to give up my house. I'm now understanding that grace and favour look very different to what I've imagined in the past.

Mary was favoured above all women and was blessed. For her it looked like rejection, isolation, stigma and possibly being stoned. Being pregnant before marriage was more than frowned upon in her culture.

God does want us to prosper, He does want to bless us and give us favour, but it might not look like we want it to. We can't afford to get caught up in this world's ideas of Christian prosperity, grace and favour. We are blessed to bless others.

Like Paul, we will go through seasons of abundance and seasons of lack. It's not how much we have that's important, it's our relationship with God and our faith in Him as provider in any situation that will bring contentment. This is an attitude that will allow us to give cheerfully and freely, not out of obligation or grudgingly.

Reaping and sowing

> *"While the earth remains, seedtime and harvest, cold and heat, winter and summer and day and night shall not cease." Genesis 8:22*

> *"Do not be deceived, God is not mocked; for whatever a man sows, that he will also reap." Galatians 6:7*

> *"But this I say: He who sows sparingly will also reap sparingly and he who sows bountifully will also reap bountifully." 2 Corinthians 9:6*

There is a principle called 'sowing and reaping.' It basically says that we reap what we sow. The Genesis passage tells us that the principle is an earthly one.

While the earth remains, seedtime and harvest will not cease.

After the earth is gone, seedtime and harvest will cease. But what will exist in its place? I believe that heaven operates with a principle of 'reaping and sowing.' It is the reverse of the earthly principle of 'sowing and reaping.'

Under the earthly principle of 'sowing and reaping,' what we receive is based on what we give. If we give time and effort in a job, we receive wages. God promises that if we sow judgement, we will reap judgement. If we sow love, we reap love. If we sow bountifully, we will reap bountifully. We reap according to what we sow.

This principle is real and valid. But I believe that as citizens of heaven we can *also* live in heavenly principles.

I believe that as Christians, not only can we benefit from the earthly principle of 'sowing and reaping,' but we can also benefit from a heavenly principle of 'reaping and sowing.'

We read the parable of the talents in Matthew 25. Jesus says that the kingdom of heaven is like a man travelling to a far country. The parable is focusing on what the kingdom of heaven is like.

The man gives his goods to his servants to look after and then leaves. They received a harvest and were expected to sow it. One servant buries what he is given and the other two use what they have and multiply it. When the lord returns he inspects what the servants have done. The two who used what they were given were congratulated but the other servant was not.

In Matthew 25:24 we read that the servant told the lord (the kingdom of heaven) that he knew the lord as a hard man who reaped where he hadn't sown and gathered where he hadn't scattered seed. The lord's (the kingdom of heaven's) answer in verse 26 agrees that he reaps where he hasn't sown and gathers where he hasn't scattered. The kingdom of heaven reaps where it hasn't sown.

Jesus says,

> *"I sent you to reap that for which you have not laboured; others have laboured and you have entered into their labours." John 4:38*

Again, Jesus is speaking of us reaping where we haven't sown.

As was mentioned earlier, Jesus lived in miracle provision. He lived in the principle of reaping and sowing. He reaped the provision of The Father and sowed into other's lives.

The feeding of the five and four thousand people are examples of that. Jesus was given loaves and fish. He didn't make them, catch them or buy them. Someone else laboured to do that. Jesus reaped things that other's had sown. He then received a miracle multiplication and sowed that food into other's lives. Many people reaped a harvest from what Jesus sowed.

We are meant to do the same. We receive miracle provision (we reap where we haven't sown) and we use it to bless others (sowing). The person we bless has then reaped where they haven't sown and they can sow so others can reap.

God loves to bless and He loves to bless through you.

Kathie Walters shared two very good examples with me where she experienced 'reaping and sowing.' I know that she has had many of these kinds of experiences.

On one occasion during 'offering time' God told Kathie to put £20 in the offering bucket after she asked Him how much to give. The place they were in had a big bucket they used to collect offering and they would sing dancing songs when giving to celebrate the goodness of God and His provision.

Kathie reached down to get her bag and found that she had left it in her car. Kathie thought that she had missed it. It couldn't be God telling her to give £20 because He would know she didn't have her bag.

She sat where she was while people were dancing around the bucket and then a child came over to her and gave her £5. She thought she may as well put that in the bucket.

On the way to the offering bucket, she bumped into another lady called Doreen and felt prompted to give Doreen the £5.

Kathie gave the £5 to Doreen and went back to her seat. On the way back, another lady stopped her and gave her £10. Kathie turned back towards the bucket but then felt she should give the £10 to a young student there. She did and went to go back to her seat.

After about a minute, a man approached Kathie and put £20 into her hands. This time she made it to the offering bucket and put the offering in. On the way out of the building, after the meeting someone ran after her and gave her £50.

The following is a direct quote from Kathie:

> *"Another time I was sitting in a Holy Ghost meeting and they took an offering. I asked the Lord what to give (I only had about £2) and he said £25. As the offering bag came down my row I reached for it with my right hand and was actually holding it when a BLIND LADY reached across two people and put £25 in my left hand! Which I put straight into the offering bag. I love how God is in everything."*

I don't know how many times I've stressed over what I've believed God has asked me to give. He told me and I tried to work out how to do it. What I should have done was just relax and let God show me how He was going to do it.

God loves to bless us and He loves to bless others through us. He is our provider and He gives us what He wants us to use and what He wants us to give.

Seed and bread

> *"Now may He who supplies seed to the sower, and bread for food, supply and multiply the seed you have sown and increase the fruits of righteousness..."* 2 Corinthians 9:10

This passage shows us that God is the one who supplies the seed and bread first. He puts us in a position where we reap even before we sow.

This is a demonstration of the grace of God. He blesses us because of who He is and not because of what we do. He provides for us because He is the Father and that's what fathers do for their children.

Some of what God provides is seed and some of it is bread. How do we know which is which? Eating seed meant for sowing is a waste of potential and burying bread just makes it mouldy. It won't grow anything.

The way we determine what is seed and what is bread is by asking God. We build intimacy with Him. We cultivate our relationship with Him so what we do stems from relationship, not ritual.

There was one time when I felt prompted by God to give $1000 to a particular person. Since that amount was over what we received in pay from various sources I thought we might be having a week of fasting as a family.

I then decided to talk some more with God to clarify what He meant. When I did He explained that He wanted me to give $500 to the person and what was left over out of the pay was to be used for food and bill paying. The $500 was seed. The rest was bread. I asked Him about the other $500 to give and He asked why I thought I was going to have all the fun. He wanted me to share the joy and provide an opportunity for others to sow seed and have it multiplied. I sent out a text to the rest of the church with what I knew God was wanting and it wasn't long before the other $500 came in.

If I hadn't spoken with God to find out what was seed and what was bread, the bread would have been wasted and others would have missed out on a great opportunity to be blessed and to be a blessing.

Ritual giving

One problem with tithing is that it can become ritualistic. We can do it from habit. It doesn't do anything to build our relationship with God. We know how much 10% of our income is so why talk to God about it?

One time early in my journey into grace I was tithing 'properly'. I had an expectation that things would work well for me, but they didn't. I didn't have the money to pay for the things that broke down.

I asked God about it, somewhat accusingly. He asked me, 'When did you speak to Me about how much to give?' He told me if I had talked to Him, He could have told me to hold on to the money, that I would need it down the track. But I hadn't. I had just tithed out of ritual, not given out of relationship.

One time I bought my son a python lolly. It was a long, soft, jube type lolly in the shape of a snake. It was a gift to him because I wanted to give him a treat.

I didn't demand or even ask for any of it back. I certainly didn't expect a 10% measurement of it. It was nice and I would have liked some but I have never set a rule that when I give my son lollies, he has to give some back to me.

Caleb broke off a bit and gave me some. He did it because he was grateful, because he loved me, because he wanted to share. It blessed me. He gave because he wanted to and liked giving. He gave out of relationship.

This gift to me was so much more meaningful than something I might have demanded from him. I think most fathers are like that. If most fathers on earth are like this, why do we believe that God is different when He is so much better than us?

Two principles

The passages from 2 Corinthians 9 show us how the two principles of 'reaping and sowing' and 'sowing and reaping' work together. The first part is that God provides seed for sowing. We reap before we sow. The second part is the sowing.

If we sow sparingly, we reap sparingly. If we sow bountifully, we reap bountifully. It means that if we sow only a small portion of what we have been given to sow, we won't reap much, on top of what God continues to provide. God does promise however, to multiply what we sow, even if it is a small amount.

If we sow all of what God has given us to sow, we will reap a lot, especially as God multiplies what we sow. There is another aspect to this though. It is the fact that what we sow, may be for someone else to reap.

Kathie Walter's story was a great example of that. God provided her something to sow. She sowed it and was given more. Eventually she sowed all the seed God gave her and He multiplied it and gave her money to keep as she was leaving the building.

We may be a vessel God is using to provide seed or bread to someone else. As God freely gives to us, we can freely give to others. We reap where we haven't sown and we sow where someone else can reap. Perhaps one of those to reap will be your pastor.

There is a place of security in giving when we receive a revelation of God as Father and provider. We can be assured that if God asks us to give everything away, He will have a way of getting what He knows we need into our hands.

Grace to give

In 2 Corinthians 8 Paul speaks of the Macedonian church. He speaks of God giving the people there a grace to give. He enabled the people, even though poor, to give beyond their ability. They had confidence in God's ability to provide for them an abundance for every good work.

While the passages from 2 Corinthians 8-9 are talking primarily about a big offering for the Jerusalem church, there are applications for us. Paul tells the Corinthian church to give as they determine in their heart.

Again, 2 Corinthians 9:7 has Paul telling the Corinthians not to give in sorrow or regret with a sour reluctance (grudgingly). He also says that they shouldn't give from a place of feeling forced to (out of necessity).

I have been told in the past that I should give a tithe because if I didn't I'd be cursed. I was also told that giving a tithe is required for a blessing. Both reasons place a sense of obligation on the giver.

Giving as we determine in our hearts promotes freedom in giving. It will also promote relationship with God as we consult Him in what we want to give. It removes the sense of obligation from having to give a certain amount.

We see very clearly the principle of 'reaping and sowing' in grace. God loved us so much that He gave us His Son, Jesus Christ. We are able to reap salvation through the death sown by Jesus. We didn't sow anything to be given it. We didn't deserve it and couldn't earn it. Salvation is a gift given freely to us.

We reaped where we didn't sow and we can sow love so others can reap that.

Giving under grace is giving in freedom. There is no obligation and no limit. It is living in the blessings of the Father because we are His children, not because we've done something to earn it. It is resting in His goodness and His ability to provide. It is giving freely, generously and abundantly even beyond what we think we are able because we trust in God and His love for us.

Why give?

After preaching messages on freedom in giving, many people have asked, 'Why should I give to the church or pastor if I don't have to?'

It's a good question. The motive behind the question will determine the kind of answer the person is willing to accept. If the person is hurt, disillusioned or offended then the question could come from resentment and a desire to hold back. The answer they may want to hear could be, 'Don't give.'

If that person suddenly doesn't want to give, it could be that their motives for giving weren't healthy and they may need to hold off giving until God has healed them. Perhaps they don't really value the church they are a part of and may need to find a place they can value and that they feel is worthy of their support. Of course there are many other reasons as well.

When I first discovered grace in giving, I never went through a period of holding back or not giving. I have known others who stopped giving because they felt cheated, controlled and manipulated. I understand that feeling and many people go through it. Jesus said that offences will come but it's what we do with offences that matter.

I went through periods of anger and judgement. I wanted to blame people but I realised that I was the one who had accepted the doctrine without thought. The truth is that very few leaders of churches deliberately set out to deceive and manipulate their congregations.

They love their congregation and want the best for them. Like Paul, they are not seeking the gift, but they are seeking the fruit that abounds to their account. In other words, they want their congregations to be blessed.

I think I continued giving because my allegiance had always been with the kingdom of God, not a person or a denomination. I love the movement I'm a part of and

I love the pastors I have sat under but I understand that none of them are perfect just like I'm not.

One reason to continue giving to the church or the pastor is that the church is a spiritual hub in the community. It is a vital part of demonstrating the love of God to those who don't know Him. Many people are blessed by the work of churches all over the world and the giver is a vital part of getting the blessing out there.

The pastor is central to the running of the church. Whether the pastor is leading the ministries themselves or overseeing and training those who are ministering, they will be more effective not having to think about secondary sources of income. If the giver values their pastor and values their church, they can help keep it running through their giving.

Sometimes a good reason to give is because ritualistic tithing may cause us to develop bad attitudes with our giving and it could cause us to become stingy. Stepping out and being generous will break that way of thinking. The generosity doesn't need to be towards a church. It could be directed towards a person, someone we know is in need.

As a pastor, why do I give?

I give to see the kingdom of God expand. I give because I love giving. I love sowing into other's lives. I love being a blessing to others. I give because I love what we are doing in our church to see our community come to Christ.

I give because God does. He gives without conditions. There have been times when I've been upset because of things that happened with the money I gave. It was used for purposes other than what I wanted. In truth, I had given the money for myself. Now I give because it's a privilege and what happens with the money is not my concern. It is a joy to give and God allows me to be a vessel of His blessing.

There are plenty more reasons for me wanting to give and I have outlined purely Biblical reasons in other areas of this book. But really, I just love giving.

What to give?

Giving is not just about money. Giving under grace is giving 100% of everything we have and all that we are. Giving and generosity are a way of living. It's a lifestyle.

Jesus told His disciples that they had received freely and that they should freely give. This statement was made in reference to healing the sick, raising the dead, cleansing lepers and casting out demons. It was not about money.

Sometimes people don't have a lot of money and it is hard for them to give even when they want to. Giving them freedom stops resentment from growing in their hearts. It also gives them opportunity to find other ways to give.

Giving can appear in many forms. People can give time, effort or materials etc., as they determine in their heart. Time, effort and materials can have as much or even more value than money. People who volunteer to minister on Sundays when they have been working all week show an amazing heart of generosity. This kind of giving is very valuable.

Other valuable giving could be cooking for people in the church who are sick, or to be a blessing in the community. It could be giving time dedicated to prayer. Retirees giving time to help at church during the week is valuable. They've finished their work life and yet they choose to continue helping and being used by God in seeing His kingdom grow.

One time after I had given a message on freedom in giving, one of my congregation members spoke to me about their giving. He was somewhat apprehensive in talking to me about it. This gentleman was retired, he was very good at fixing things and he often used his own materials when he helped around the church.

He asked me if it was OK if all he could give was his time, effort and materials that he had accumulated over time. I told him that it would be OK if he didn't even give that. I also told him how much I appreciated everything he did do around the church.

I watched as he visibly relaxed, breathing a sigh of relief. He then explained to me that pastors he had been under in the past had told him that he should do all the things he was doing around the church, but he still had to give the tithes and offerings because it was only the money that counted with God.

This man had lived under a cloud of oppression coming to church because he felt he couldn't please God with what he was able to give. He was left in doubt about his relationship with the Father and was never really comfortable being in His presence. After speaking with him, the heaviness left and he enjoyed being in church again.

While I know that the pastor who told this man those things does not represent the majority of pastors, it does highlight the responsibility we have to teach the truth. To do otherwise will bring people into bondage in their relationship with God, rather than freedom.

Intimacy in giving

Living in grace means walking in the Spirit. We can only walk effectively in the Spirit when we cultivate intimacy with God. Our giving needs to spring out of the intimacy we have with God. Our giving comes from walking in the Spirit.

It is by spending time with God, sitting at His feet and receiving, that we will walk in the revelation that we hear and know His voice. John 10 has a number of references to Jesus' sheep hearing His voice. He doesn't speak about His sheep having to learn to hear and know His voice. If we are His sheep, we just will hear and know His voice, because that is what His sheep do.

I have spoken to many people who say they don't hear God. The truth is that they do hear from God, they just don't realise it. His message can come to us through dreams, visions, the Bible, prophecies, unexpected thoughts, as well as feelings and impressions, among other things.

Spending time with Him and becoming intimate with Him, through the Word and the Spirit, will enable us to better recognise the methods He is using to talk to us.

One problem that can arise when asking God questions is that we can have a preconceived idea of what His answer will be. That expectation may hinder us from hearing God's real answer.

Gavin Tooley gave the following example:

> *"If I ask God, 'What season do I pick apples from an orange tree?' I am expecting an answer of one of four seasons. God could actually be saying, 'Apples don't grow on orange trees' but I could miss it because He hasn't answered with one of the four answers I was expecting."*

If I am considering how much I am meant to give, but I have an expectation of 10% I may not be ready to receive His answer if it's different to my expectation. He might actually be saying, 'Give nothing this week' or 'Give it all this week.' I may miss it because it's not what I am expecting.

If we don't have an understanding of our Father as Provider, even when we hear His voice, we may not receive it or follow it out of fear. Allowing God to reveal Himself as 'The Lord Will Provide' will enable us to be open to receive whatever answer He gives in relation to giving, and be responsive to it through faith.

Be free

Our Father is a good provider. He gives good things to those who ask. He loves His children and He blesses them. We can trust Him.

Some time ago I felt God leading me to start a business. I assumed that because He wanted me to start the business, He was going to make me a multi-millionaire. I was wrong. Actually I was very wrong.

God didn't tell me what would happen when I started the business only that He wanted me to start it. If He told me what would happen I may not have started it. God is pretty smart that way.

The business made no money, my wife and I went into debt, we lost the money from the house we had to sell and our marriage nearly fell apart. At some points we had to make choices between buying food and paying rent because we couldn't do both.

I continued to tithe and give offerings in spite of the financial difficulties.

My sense of shame and guilt increased when I didn't give and I found myself making promises to God when I missed the tithe that I would repay Him later. Stress increased with the pressure to give, buy food and pay bills.

Eventually I let the business go and went back to teaching. It was a hard decision because I had left teaching earlier due to stress and having a breakdown. After a number of years we did get back out of debt and buy another house.

Our combined income was around $140,000 per year and we were getting ahead. I was learning about giving under grace and then we accepted God's invitation to begin pastoring. Our combined income suddenly dropped to nearly a quarter of what it was. We had to sell our house again and things looked like they were going to go back to where we were. But there was a difference.

I was free. I gave generously and abundantly and I loved doing it. My wife and I didn't fight about finances. We trusted God as our provider. When God said to hold off giving for a particular week I was disappointed but I felt no shame or guilt. I felt no pressure. Every time I gave, I gave with delight.

After the first year of pastoring the church I looked at our personal income and expenditure and found that we had paid out around $7,000 more than had come in as income. We hadn't gone backwards and so $7,000 had appeared from nowhere. God provided.

After five years our income hasn't changed and yet Tania and I are doing more and experiencing life like we never did when we were on the higher income. We are giving more and we don't know how, but we don't bother asking.

God is good and He has set us free to give out of faith in Him as provider. He wants you to be free as well.

Conclusion

Some time ago, God asked me to give a $100 and at that time it was beyond what I thought I could pay. I had bills that needed to be paid and as I was working as a casual teacher, I had no guarantee of income. I balked at the idea.

God asked me if I was prepared to practice what I preached. There was no condemnation in the question. It was just a question. I knew that if I didn't, God wouldn't love me less. I knew I wasn't going to be cursed. I knew blessing wouldn't stop.

I gave the money God asked me to give. A day later I was given a number of day's casual work. I had enough money to pay the bills and more left over. I asked God if the work was a reward for being obedient or for exercising my faith. Was it multiplication on what I gave? He said that it wasn't.

He told me that He knew the work was coming whether I gave or not. The work was a blessing because He loved me. Giving was just an opportunity to be a blessing to someone else. He said it will always remind me that when I give as He asks, I will be secure that He will provide.

As a pastor who has freed his congregation from giving tithes, I have had ample opportunity to see God provide. People do give. They give cheerfully, they give abundantly and generously. They give freely. Sometimes I don't think it's enough, but God helps me keep my mouth closed when I think that, and God always provides the shortfall.

People give, not because they have to, but because they want to. They want to be a part of what God is doing here. They love being a part of how we help our community. They want to bless the pastor. They want to bless each other. They want to pour the love of God out on others in whatever way God asks them to. His sons are free.

One person in our congregation is quite well off. They had been the financial backstop for the last pastors. When my wife and I arrived, this person told me that if we needed anything for the church, to tell them. Even though this person liked to give, they had felt the pressure of being the church's and the pastor's provider for some time.

I didn't want to rob them of the joy of giving, but I knew it was not what God wanted. I said to them that I wouldn't tell them when we needed anything. I said they needed to talk to God about it.

I have stuck with this and watched the person grow. They have learnt to hear God's voice in a way they never believed they could. The pressure for keeping the church going was lifted off their shoulders and opened the door for God to provide in so many other ways.

I like being able to look to God as my provider. Even though He may use the church to provide, it is still Him who provides for me. Sometime I may leave this church (I hope not, but that is up to God), and if I do, I can leave knowing that the church owes me nothing.

I came here to preach the gospel and I know I've done it free of charge. I didn't come here looking for a job and job security. I came to fulfil God's call on my life and to feed His sheep.

The last point to make is this: do whatever you have the faith to do.

It takes faith to rest in the security of God as provider. When I tithed I knew I could use 90% of my income for what I wanted. Living with the understanding that

100% of my income is available for God to use is just plain scary to me. I need more faith to do that than to tithe.

I don't want this book to be a stumbling block for anyone. I have recorded what I believe is the truth about tithing and giving but you need to ask yourself what you have the faith for. It is up to you to work out whether your faith allows you to give or to tithe.

There are some who read this and will not receive a revelation of the freedom we have under grace in terms of giving. I urge that person, rather than go against your conscience, continue to tithe.

God never says anywhere in His word not to give. What is important is the heart attitude we give with.

God responds to faith. If your faith says to tithe, then tithe. God will honour that. If your faith says you can simply give, then give in freedom. God will honour that. This book is not to tell people what they have to do, but to open their eyes to what may be possible in God.

I believe that the Bible teaches us to give, to support our local part of the body of Christ, to bless others and to trust in His ability to provide. I believe that we are called to greater depths of freedom in Christ, and one of those areas is in giving. I believe that He is calling His people to be givers not tithers.

Bibliography

Morley, Brian K. 1996. *"Tithe, Tithing."* In *Baker Theological Dictionary of the Bible*. Edited by Walter A. Elwell. Grand Rapids: Baker Books House.

Edited by Oppenheim, A. Leo, Gelb, Ignace J., Jacobsen, Thorkild, Landsberger, Benno. 1958. *The Assyrian Dictionary of the Oriental Institute of the University of Chicago (Vol 4, "E")*. Chicago: The Oriental Institute https://oi.uchicago.edu/sites/oi.uchicago.edu/files/uploads/shared/docs/cad_e.pdf

Jacobs, Louis. 2011. "Tithing." *My Jewish Learning*. Reprinted from *"The Jewish Religion: A Companion."* By Rabbi Louis Jacob. Oxford: Oxford University Press. http://www.myjewishlearning.com/article/tithing/ Accessed June 17, 2015.

Melamed, Eliezer Rabbi. 2013. "Judaism: Wealth Through Tithing." *Israel National News*, August 4, 2013. Accessed June 17, 2015. http://www.israelnationalnews.com/Articles/Article.aspx/13645#.VYE0z_mqqko

Brown-Driver-Briggs. 2002 *Hebrew and English Lexicon* Unabridged, Electronic Database, by BibleSoft, Inc, as used in www.biblesuite.com/hebrew/5186 and www.biblesuite.com/hebrew/4941

Gill, John. 1763. *Matthew 23:23: Gill's Exposition of the Entire Bible*. Public Domain. Accessed June 17, 2015. http://biblehub.com/commentaries/gill/matthew/23.htm

Tractate Ma'aseroth, Chapter 1, Mishna 1. Accessed June 17, 2015. http://www.hebrewbooks.org/pagefeed/hebrewbooks_org_9 675_339.pdf

The Holy Bible

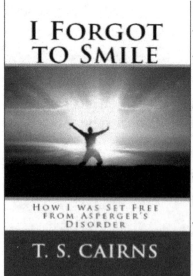

This book is a powerful testimony of how Tim Cairns was set free from a curse that had been in his family for generations. It is funny and informative and it   demonstrates the power, love and grace of Jesus.

This book can be purchased at the following websites:

http://www.scorebrowniepoints.com.au/downloads/i-forgot-to-smile/

http://www.kathiewaltersministry.com/apps/webstore/products/show/5380827

http://www.amazon.com/Forgot-Smile-Free-Aspergers-Disorder/dp/1888081163

About the Author

Tim is married to Tania and they have three children: Shantelle, Candice and Caleb. Tim and Tania also have one granddaughter, Mercy, who they intend to spoil terribly. Tim and Tania pastor two churches in the Hunter Valley, New South Wales, Australia.

Tim has had a passion for the Word of God since a very young age. He would constantly question his parents in regards to the meaning of passages. They were really glad when he got his hands on a Strong's Concordance.

Tim trained as a Science Teacher and holds a Bachelor of Education in Science. He taught in a number of schools and caused them to be evacuated repeatedly when he blew things up. Tim tried many avenues to help God bring finances into the kingdom. In each case he found out his gifting lay in other areas and that God didn't need his help anyway. He has been involved in leading ministries in churches for around twenty years and finds it more successful and less stressful when he just does what God tells him to do.

Tim's website is www.scorebrowniepoints.com.au. The website is dedicated to exploring grace in relationships with our spouse and with God. Tim has other books for sale on this website and will continue to add new ones.

While Tim loves writing, he also loves researching the Word, finding truth and presenting it in a way that everybody can understand.